SOCIAL MOBILITY AMONG SCHEDULED CASTE WOMEN IN INDIA

Social Mobility Among Scheduled Caste Women in India

(A Study of Kerala)

Dr. LEELA VISWANATH

UPPAL PUBLISHING HOUSE
NEW DELHI—110002

UPPAL PUBLISHING HOUSE
3, Ansari Road, Daryaganj, New Delhi-110002
Phones : 3273756, 2242884.

First Edition 1993
ISBN 81-85565-33-3

Printed in India

Published by B.S. Uppal for Uppal Publishing House
3, Ansari Road, Daryaganj, New Delhi-110002
and Printed at Sainion Printary, Delhi - 110032.

Foreword

This book on "Social mobility Among Scheduled Caste Women in Kerala", based on extensive field study and rigorous analysis, is a welcome addition to the existing literature on women's studies. Though studies on Scheduled castes in various parts of India are abundant, seldom has been the focus on women. Scheduled Caste Women are often doubly handicapped. On the one hand they belong to the socially and economically backward stratum of society and, on the other hand, because they belong to weaker sex, they are subjected to exploitation. The constitutional guarantee of equality and the legal enactments, welfare measures and development programmes, intronuced during the post-Independence period, have ameliorated the hardships and improved the position of Scheduled Castes to some extent. However, research studies on the improvement in the position of scheduled caste women, especially on their social mobility, are quite scanty.

Based on a sample of 450 women belonging to two geneations from three districts of Kerala, Leela Viswanath has examined the extent of social mobility among the scheduled caste women. She has also analysed the factors contributing to such mobility the major among them being education, modern occupation, changing inter-caste relations and change in attitudes and levels of aspirations. Two case studies on three generations of women enrich the in-depth knowledge on the various dimensions of mobility and change among them. The study reveals distinct patterns of inter-generational mobility in several areas.

The rigid caste system, with its acute discriminatory and oppressive features, has been undergoing gradual but progressive transformation in Kerala, thanks to various factors like the early missionary efforts, social reform movements, land reforms, progressive and protective laws, and consistently high investments by the state in literacy and education.

No wonder the position of Scheduled Caste women has improved considerably, between the two generations studies by Leela Viswanath. The Kerala situation is, however, a typical of other parts of the country. Many more similar studies are required to develop a proper understanding on the various factors and patterns of social mobility among Scheduled Caste Women.

The findings of the present volume have implications for policies and programmes for the Scheduled Castes in general and their women in particular. I have great pleasure in recommending this book to social scientists and policy planners, especially those dealing with the weaker sections of society and with women's empowerment programmes.

Dr. P.K.B. NAYAR

Preface

The present study aims to identify the factors responsible for Social mobility among scheduled caste women in Kerala and the areas in which such mobility is distinctly marked.

Dealing with factors influencing education, the author finds considerable educational mobility between the generations and that there is definite improvement in the educational level. The trend on occupational mobility shows that intra generational mobility among mothers is horizantal while in the next generation it is to some extent, upward and vertical, although the transitum does not follow a uniform pattern. The study also focuses on mobility in area like interpersonal relations and analysis attitudinal differences in regard to age at marriage, widom marriage, dowry etc, among the two generations of scheduled caste women. Over all, the results show social mobility among scheduled caste women in Kerala.

The book is likely to probe useful to academicians, policy makers and planners.

I must acknowledge my sense of deep gratitude to individuals and institutions who enabled me to complete the study.

I am grateful to Dr. (Mrs.) M. Indu Kumari, Reader, Department of Sociology, University of Kerala, also my guide, for her guidance and forthright, but valuable comments. She has been a constant source of inspiration and patence itself to me and words are never enough to express my gratitude to her.

I am indebted to Dr. P.K.B. Nayar, Professor and Head, Department of Sociology, University of Kerala, for providing me with all the research facilities.

My sincere thanks are due to Shri. T.K. Srinivasan Unnithan, Reader, Department of Statistics, University of Kerala, for giving statistical guidance for my study.

I am grateful to I.C.S.S.R and University of Kerala for porividing financial assistance to me.

I will be failing in my duty, if I don't express my gratitude to the Harijan Welfare Department, and Libraries of Department of Sociology, University Library, Social Science Documentation Centre, New Delhi, Centre for Development Studies, Trivandrum who have rendered great help and facilities for consulations and secondary data collections. I owe a dedt of gratitude to all of them.

I pay regards to my husband Mr. N. Viswanathan Nair who has fully co-operated with me in preparing the manuscript, and who gave me support at all, occosions.

I am indebted to all my respondent, without whose co-operation and sincerity this study would have been drowned to be a failure.

Lastly my personal thanks are due to Mr. B.S.Uppal, for taking keen interest in the publication of this book.

Dr. LEELA VISWANATH

Contents

List of Tables

CHAPTER I

Introduction

SCHEDULED CASTES IN INDIA

Caste system is a unique feature of Indian society. Caste is a very complex phenomenon and it acts as a principle of social stratification. The traditional features of caste system are :

(1) Endogamy,

(2) hierarchy,

(3) restrictions on commensal relations between castes,

(4) restrictions on choice of occupation,

(5) civil and religious disabilities and privileges of certain groups, and

(6) untouchability".[1]

According to varna theory, there are four types of varnas such as Brahmins, Kshatriyas, Vaishyas, and Sudras. It was

1. G.S. Ghurye, *Caste, Class and Occupation,* Popular Book Depot, Bombay ; 1961, p. 2.

considered that Brahmins were originated from the mouth of Brahma, Kshatriyas from the arms, Vaishyas from the thighs, Sudras from the feet. Since Sudras were supposed to have sprung from the lowest part of the body, they were assigned the lowest position in the varna hierarchy. The scheduled castes of today belong to sudra varna.

It is well known that the lower castes had no place in the ancient fourfold varna system and were referred to as untouchables, depressed classes, or exterior castes. Discrimination was the main feature of social structure and status was determined by birth. Due to their very low social and ritual status in the traditional Hindu society, they have remained extremely poor backward for centuries.

In the year 1901, Risely, the Census Commissioner of India, attempted for the first time, to classify the Hindu castes according to their social standing. Accordingly, the population was divided into the following seven categories ;

(1) Brahmins,
(2) castes other than Brahmins who rank above the clean sudras,
(3) clean sudras,
(4) clean castes served by the degraded Brahmins,
(5) castes other than group, whose water is not taken;
(6) unclean castes ;
(7) unclean feeders.

In the Census of 1911, an enquiry was instituted to ascertain the castes and tribes which suffered specified religious and social disabilities. Although the term depressed class has been mentioned in the Census Report of 1921, the castes constituting the depressed class have not been defined. The term "Depressed Castes" was used before 1930, but since the enactment of the Government of India Act of 1935, they have consistently referred to as scheduled castes".[2] Harold Issacs is of the opinion that the term "Depressed classes" was introduced some time late in the last century, in British officials records. It was only in 1932, that this word was officially defined as the "untouchables". In the various Indian languages they were known by many versions of words that mean "untouchables" or "out caste", of variations thereof; Panchamas, Atishudras, Avarnas, Antyajas, Nama Sudras, etc. One also comes across words such as "Pariahs", "Unseables" and "Unapproachables". In 1933 Gandhi coined the new term, "Harijans", meaning "children of God".[3] Dr. Ambedkar proposed the words 'protestant Hindus' or 'No-conformist Hindus'. Finally, as recommended by the Simon Commission, the term, "Scheduled Castes" was adopted by the Government.

The term "Scheduled Castes" has not been defined any where in the Constitution. Article 341 of the Constitution reads as follows : "Scheduled Caste" mean such castes, races or tribes, parts or groups within such castes, races or tribes as are deemed under Article 341 to be the scheduled castes for the purpose of the Constitution of India.[4] To put it briefly, it may be said that all the "Depressed Classes" are Harijans. All the Harijans denote untouchables and are scheduled castes.

There were many social and legal restrictions and other disabilities that were traditionally associated with the scheduled caste people. They were denied access to religious places, and to use water from public wells, not allowed to attend schools and had to remain outside because their contact should pollute upper caste Hindus. Besides these, they were debarred from using public roads and forced to live on the outskirts of higher caste's residential area, thus creating hindrance to their

2. L.P. Vidyarthi and N. Mishra, *Harijan Today*, Classical Publications, New Delhi ; 1970, pp. 2-3.

3. Harold R. Isaacs, *India's Ex-untouchables*, Asia Publishing House, Bombay, 1965, p. 36.

mobility. They had no share in the social, political and judiciary powers. "The early reform movements such as Arya Samaj, Brahma Samaj, Prarthana Samaj, and National Social Conference were induced with a liberal ideology of social welfare and upliftment of backward classes. The early social reform movements were concerned with two major questions : the emancipation of women and the amelioration of the condition of a section of society called the depressed classes. The basic problems of these depressed castes were economic, educational, political, ritual and civic disabilities of varying degrees."[5]

The efforts of social reformers and politicians helped a lot in improving scheduled caste's status and also their civic position. Gandhiji was the first Indian to carry on an organised movement against the atrocities practised towards the depressed castes. He insisted that the untouchables should be treated as Hindus with all the rights which the caste Hindus enjoyed and as such he paved the way to social mobility among Scheduled Castes. Gandhi's efforts in securing social mobility for the Harijans in the economic, political, occupational and religious fields had been widely acknowledged".[6]

"The agrarian struggles and social reform movements that took place in India in the latter half of the last century and early decades of the present century, and the independence movement threatened the old order based on custom and introduced ideas of protest and challenge instead of acceptance and submissiveness. The struggles threw up many leaders from the lower strata. It was the agitations and movements that they led that compelled the authorities to initiate many of the

4. *Constitution of India*, Eastern Book Company, Lucknow ; 1977, p. 128.
5. M.S.A. Rao, *Social Movements and Social Transformation*, Mac Millan and Company of India Limited, Delhi ; 1979, p. J.
6. P.G. Shaw, *Report of the Seminar or Casteism and Removal of Untouchability*, Bombay ; Published by the Indian Conference of Social Work, 1955, p. 71.

measures which in later years were absorbed into the welfare policies for the poor and deprived sections'.[7]

The appointment of a Commissioner for Scheduled Castes and Scheduled Tribes to look after the interests and welfare of these people, was a landmark in the history of the country. The Untouchability Offence Act, 1955 or Act No. XXII of 1955 was still further step towards the removal of the social disabilities of the Scheduled Castes. Under this Act, the religious disabilities, and social disabilities are treated as offences punishable.

In the field of education, occupation, and income, there are many programmes implemented by the Government for the development of Scheduled Castes. Special programmes in educational field, special recruitment in the Government Departments for Scheduled Castes etc., were contributing to the mobility among Scheduled Castes.

Demographic Composition of Scheduled Castes

In India, the proportion of scheduled castes population is increasing. Among the scheduled castes, the sex-ratio was characterised by male domination. The proportion of scheduled castes population in India was 14.7 per cent in 1961. Among them, 50.03 per cent were males. According to 1971 Census, the scheduled castes population constituted 14.60 per cent, and 51.68 per cent of them were males. The 1981 Census data shows that 15.7 per cent of the population is scheduled castes while that of 51.75 per cent were males. The following Table shows the scheduled caste population in India for the last three decades.

In Kerala, scheduled castes constitute 10.02 per cent of the total population according to 1981 Census as against 8.30 per cent as per 1971 Census and 8 5 per cent as per 1961

7. Saradamoni, *Emergence of a Slave Caste*, People's Publishing House, New Delhi ; 1980, p. X.

TABLE 1

Scheduled Caste Population in India*

Year	*Male*	*Female*	*Total*
1961	50.73%	49.27%	14.70%
1971	51.68%	48.32%	14.60%
1981	51.75%	48.25%	15.74%

* *Census of India*, 1961, 1971, 1981. Union Primary Census Abstract, Series I, Part II, B (ii).

Census. Among these scheduled castes in Kerala the sex ratio was characterised by dominance of female i.e., 50.54 per cent according to 1981 Census whereas 50.40 per cent and 50.2 per cent as per 1961 Census and 1971 Census. The following Table shows the rate of scheduled caste population in Kerala for the last three decades.

TABLE 2

Scheduled Castes Population in Kerala*

Year	*Male*	*Female*	*Total*
1961	49.60%	50.40%	8.50%
1971	49.98%	50.02%	8.30%
1981	49.46%	50.54%	10.02%

* Census of India 1961, 1971, 1981.

Literacy Rate of Scheduled Castes in India

In India education is considered as the most important media for social mobility. Education helps to acquire high social status through educational, economic and occupational mobility. Education is the harbinger of change in the form of new life styles, new value systems and new institutional matrix. "In the context of scheduled castes who were hitherto largely illiterate and ignorant, education has most significant role to play. The economic distress in which the Harijan community has to live and the stigma attached to their polluting occupations could be overcome only through education. Education also provides them the necessary skill, training and aptitude to gain better economic opportunities".[8]

The literacy rate was very low for scheduled castes probably because they were prohibited from learning since ages. Even castes in Sudra Varna which were above scheduled castes in caste hierarchy were not allowed to take education.

It is being increasingly believed that education can be a powerful means to ameliorate the suffering Harijans and for overcoming the social, psychological and economic barriers under which they have been reeling since long. The conscientiousness for upliftment, through educating Harijans emerged during

TABLE 3

Literacy Level of Scheduled Castes in India*

Year	*Male*	*Female*	*Total*
1961	16.96%	3.29%	10.27%
1971	22.43%	6.45%	14.67%
1891	31.12%	10.82%	21.38%

* *Census of India*, a. 1961, b. 1971, c. 1981.

(a) *Union. Primary Abstract Series I*, Part IIA(ii), p. xxxii.

(b) *Special tables on Scheduled Castes and Scheduled Tribes Series 9*, Kerala Part VA.

(c) *Census Abstract Scheduled Castes series I*, Part II B(i).

8. M.S. Showeb, *Education and Mobility among Harijans*, Vohra Publishers and Distributors, Allahabad ; 1986, p. 19.

the nineteenth century and is still on. The idea originated with the coming of missionaries with the East India Company".[9]

Literacy among the scheduled castes, on the whole, is still very low. The rate of progress in education of scheduled caste in India is quite clear from the following Table.

It would be seen that the rate of progress for males was slightly higher than the level of educational progress of the female population.

In Kerala

Like in other parts of India, in Kerala also the Harijans suffered a lot at the hands of high castes. Under the cover of purity and pollution which was imposed on the untouchables by the high caste, society denied their education and admission to public places. Education for scheduled castes in general, and women in particular, were totally restricted. "Traditionally, in Kerala the structural distance prevalent between castes was translatable into spatial distance. It was thus possible to measure the social status of a caste by finding out how closely it was entitled to approach the Nambudiri Brahmin".[10]

The famous Vykom Satyagraha which was started in 1924, and the Temple Entry Proclamation Act of 1936 helped a lot for the upliftment of lower castes in the society. The untouchability Act of 1955 came into force in June 1st 1955 which checked to a certain extent the behaviour and treatment of high castes towards lower castes.

In Kerala, the State Government took special steps in extending free education to the scheduled castes at primary level. In a study about scheduled castes, N.D. Kamble revealed that

9. B.R. Goyal, *Educating Harijans*, The Academic Press, Haryana; 1981, p. 24.
10. A. Aiyappan, *Social Revolution in a Kerala Village*, Asia Publishing House, Bombay ; 1965, p. vii.

"Kerala, Maharashtra and Karnataka have relatively more facilities for education, as a split over effect, scheduled castes also got education. In Kerala the educational facilities are so many as compared to many regions in India".[11]

"Though considerable progress has been achieved in educational field among certain sections of scheduled castes and scheduled tribes population, the progress is very poor among a sizeable portion of the population. The sections which have not achieved remarkable progress are those which were in the lowest rank of the social system in the past. It may take a longer time for these sections to be free from the disabilities and handicaps to which they were subjected to and to become equal to others".[12]

TABLE 4

Literacy Rate of Scheduled Castes in Kerala.*

Year	*Male*	*Female*	*Total*
1961	30.50%	19.10%	24.40%
1971	47.10%	33.42%	41.81%
1981	62.33%	49.73%	56.00%

* *Census of India,* (a) 1961, (b) 1971, (c) 1981.

(a) *Primary Census, Abstract Scheduled Castes series I, Part II (B) (ii) 1981.*

(b) *Special tables on Scheduled Castes and Scheduled Tribes Census of India, Series 9,* Kerala, Part V.A. 1979.

(c) *Union Primary Census Abstract.* Series I, India : 1961. Part II-A (ii).

11. N.D. Kamble, *The Scheduled Castes,* Asia Publishing House, New Delhi ; 1982, p. 51.
12. Government of Kerala, *Report of Commissioner on the Socio-Economic Conditions of Scheduled Castes and Scheduled Tribes,* Vol. I, Part I, 1982, p. 24.

According to 1961 and 1971 Census, the percentage of literacy among the scheduled castes was 24.4 per cent and 41.81 per cent, but it has risen to 56 per cent as per 1981 Census. It was found that rate of progress for males was higher than the level of progress of females in Kerala.

Scheduled Caste Women in Kerala

The treatment that the scheduled caste women received from the higher castes was very miserable in ancient times. The status of scheduled caste women, both in rural and urban areas, was very low. In early days, education was strictly prohibited for women in general, and scheduled caste women in particular. They had their own particular habits, customs and way of life. Even in the case of their dressing pattern, there was difference from that of high caste women. The governmental efforts, social reform movements and continuous efforts of social leaders helped them to improve their image. Consequently, their position in the present society.

Traditional restrictions on women's education, and especially education of scheduled caste women had a hindering influence on their status in society. The level of literacy among the Harijan community has been lowest in the case of Harijan women. Scheduled caste women in the past, had their own traditional occupations. They served as agriculture labourers and performed other mental jobs such as midwifery and scavenging, which do not require any formal education.

Governmental efforts, new socio-economic developments, and equal opportunities for education, had created new attitudes and aspirations among Scheduled Caste women. The parents began to develop favourable attitude towards their children's education. Education is given due emphasis as a powerful instrument for changing Scheduled Caste women's subordinate position. Social status and educational level are obviously related with each other.

As a consequence of the welfare measures provided by the government in the form of educational facilities and job opportunities, the status and style of life of the Scheduled Caste women have improved a lot, when compared to earlier periods.

Welfare Measures for Scheduled Castes in Kerala

Welfare measures for Scheduled Castes in Kerala have a long history. The rulers of the erstwhile Travancore had initiated as early as in the beginning of 19th century, social reform movement with the objective of removing social and economic disabilities of the 'depressed castes'. "Proclamations were issued in 1818, 1853, and 1855, abolishing all forms of slavery and imposing severe punishments and offenders. This was followed by orders passed in 1870, prohibiting the use of derogatory terms (indicating their serfdom) against the Scheduled Castes in public documents. The 'depressed castes' were permitted to enter Government offices, in the same year"[13] Schools were started for the benefit of the Depressed Castes, in 1884, and in the following year scholarships were instituted for them.

Since 1950, there has been radical change in the approach of the Government, towards the betterment of the conditions of Scheduled Castes. Introduction of universal adult franchise, compulsary elementary education, provision of social justice, equality and freedom and prevention of exploitation were some measures which has benefitted the Scheduled Castes more than group of citizens. Translation of various constitutional provisions into actions resulted in inclusion of several schemes in the various five year plans, the most important of them being the educational policy for the Scheduled Castes. The significance attached to education by the Government, in bringing out

13. L.A. Krishna Iyer, *Social History of Kerala*, Vol. II, Book Centre Publications, Madras, 1968, p. 62.

socio-economic development among Scheduled Castes is reflected in the following observation of the Commissioner for Scheduled Castes and Scheduled Tribes. "The spread of education among the weaker sections of society is an essential prerequisite to their all round development and to assure them benefits of various safeguards provided under the constitution".[14] The importance given to education is strengthened again in the following statement of the Report of the Commissioner for Scheduled Castes and Scheduled Tribes. "If the Directive Principles of State Policy that the operation of the economic system should not result in the concentration of wealth and means of production to the common deteriment is to be given practical shape, the state should intensify its efforts to offer greater educational opportunities to these communities".[15]

Educational facilities find a priority in the programmes of Scheduled Castes and Scheduled Tribes Development Departments of the State Government, for a long time. Besides, the Harijan Welfare Department has launched various other schemes to improve the economic, social and health conditions of the Scheduled Castes. A brief description of these schemes are given below :

Pre-primary Education

Nursury schools were started in various parts of the state, to provide opportunities for parents belonging to Scheduled Castes and Scheduled Tribes communities to send their children for nursury. There were 56 nursury schools and 100 Balawadi-

14. Government of India, *Reports of the Commissioner for Scheduled Castes and Scheduled Tribes*, 1962-63, Manager of Publication, New Delhi, p. 50.

15. Government of India, *Report of the Commissioner for Scheduled Castes and Scheduled Tribes*, Manager of Publication, New Delhi ; 1965.

cum-feeding centres (as on 1-4-1980) under the Scheduled Caste Department.

Stipends and Grants

Monetary incentives such as lumpsum grants and monthly stipends have been provided to the Scheduled Castes, for their education from standard I onwards. The rates have been revised from time to time. In addition, the Scheduled caste students are also exempted from payment of any kind of fees.

Residential Facilities

To these Scheduled Caste students who are not able to attend educational institutions as day-scholars are provided with free hostel accomodation and boarding.

Reservation of Seats in Educational Institutions

20 per cent of seats in all colleges are reserved for Scheduled Caste students.

In addition to the above, the Government is also providing free coaching facilities for the Scheduled Caste candidates to prepare them for services of all India competitive examinations.

Scholarships to Brilliant Students

In order to improve the standard of education of the Scheduled Caste students, the Harijan Welfare Department has also implemented various training programmes and scholarships. Students who score 60 per cent or more marks at the S.S.L.C., Pre-Degree, Degree, and Post-Graduate levels are eligible to draw scholarships at the rate of Rs. 150, Rs. 165, Rs. 225 and Rs. 750 respectively.

Those who are doing professional courses like Medicine and Engineering, are being provided with reference books, so as to improve their educational facilities.

The Harijan Welfare Department has set up various Industrial Training Centres, for providing the Scheduled Castes with training in their traditional work like carpentary, weaving, sewing, mat weaving, tailoring, cane work etc. These trainees are given a stipend of Rs. 90 each per month in the first year and Rs. 130 each per month in the second year.

Production-cum-Training Centre

After the training, these persons are given special training for 2 years, during which, they will be absorbed in any of the training centres and are given salary according to the work done.

Self-Emloyment Scheme

The Harijan Walefare Department is also giving financial assistance to those who have completed training, in setting up independent industry or, other business.

B. ECONOMIC

Interest Free Loans

The Scheduled Caste people are also eligible for a loan of upto Rs. 15,000, interest free loan for starting small scale industry or other business.

Those, who are received training in tailoring, are provided with sewing machines, on instalment basis.

Loan for Scheduled Caste Advocates

Scheduled Caste advocates, who receive an annual income of less than Rs. 3000/- are given loan for practising law.

Co-operative societies are also set up at different parts of the state for helping the trainees find jobs according to their training.

Block level Extension Programme

Several information centres are set up at Development Blocks through which the Scheduled Caste people receive guidelines and advises for their social, economic and educational upliftment.

Recreational Facilities

As a part of recreational facilities, the Harijan Walfare Department has given aid to set up facilities, many Colour Television sets in various Scheduled Caste colonies.

Seasonal Day Care Centre

Many Seasonal Day Care Centres are also functioning in Kuttanadu, Trichur and Ponnani, for looking after the children of financially backward scheduled caste agricultural workers.

C. HEALTH AND HOUSING

Housing Grant

Harijan Welfare Department is also providing housing loans to Scheduled Caste people who have land and annual income of less than Rs. 4,200/-.

House Building Loans

Scheduled Castes are eligible for a loan upto Rs. 10,000/- interest free, for building house.

Drinking Water Facilities

Wells and tube-wells are also being dug in order to provide the Scheduled Caste colonies with drinking water.

House Thatching Grant

Funds are also attached to the Scheduled Caste people for thatching and tiling their houses.

Inter-caste Marriage grant

The inter-caste couples, who are socially isolated and are

struggling for livelihood, are provided with Rs. 2000/- per couple, in order to help them find a job.

The Harijan Welfare Department also gives a grant of Rs, 100/- in each to victims of accidents like earth quake, fire and epidermis.

The Scheduled Caste people are also eligible for T.A. for for attending interviews and competitive examinations.

Social Mobility-Theoretical Framework

The concept of 'social mobility' in our study is adopted mainly from Sorokin and Bernard Barber. The following is a brief analysis of their contributions to the concept. According to Sorokin, 'social mobility in its broadest sense is the shifting of people in social space". He was not, however, interested in movements of individuals but in social metabolism, in the consequences of such movements for social groups differently located in the social structure. Sorokin presents the innovative idea that social mobility does not primarily concern the placement of individuals but is to be understood as exchange between social groups. By fostering the circulation of individuals in social space, such exchange increases or decreases the specific weight and power of the groups and strata between which they move'.[16]

"Sorokin has divided social mobility into two principal types : horizontal mobility and vertical mobility. By horizontal social mobility or shifting, is meant the transition of an individual or social object from one social group to another situated on the same level. By vertical social mobility is meant the relations involved in a transition of an individual (or a social object) from one stratum to another. The vertical social mobility indicates a change in status, but in

16. L.A. Coser, *Masters of Sociological Thought*, Harcount Brace, Jovanovich, Inc. New York, 1977, pp. 473-476.

horizontal social mobility, no change in status is found. According to the direction of the transition, there are two types of vertical social mobility, ascending and descending or social climbing and social sinking. According to the nature of the stratification, there are ascending and descending currents of economic, political and occupational mobility, not to mention other less important types. The ascending currents exist in two principal forms as infiltration of the individuals of a lower stratum into an existing higher one and as a creation of a new group by such individuals, and the insertion of such a group into a higher stratum instead of or side by side with, the existing groups of this stratum. Correspondingly, the descending current has also two principal forms ; the first consists in a dropping of individuals from a higher social position into an existing lower one without a degradation or disintegration of the higher group to which they belonged to the second is manifested in a degradation of a social group as a whole, in an abasement of its rank among other groups, or in its disintegration as a social unit".[17]

Bernard Barber defined mobility as "a movement either upward or downward between higher and lower social classes or more precisely movement between one relatively full time, functionally significant social role and another that is evaluated as either higher or lower. This movement is to be conceived as a process occuring overtime, with individuals (and their family units) moving from one role and social class position to another because of what they have done or what has happened to them in various kinds of social interaction, such as in their family or in their work organisation, or during war of socio-economic expansions in their society".[18]

17. P.A. Sorokin, *Social and Cultural Mobility*, Free Press America, 1952, pp. 133-34.

18. Bernard Barber, *Social Stratification*, A Comparative Analysis of Structure and Process, Harcount Brace and Co., New York. 1957, pp. 356-57.

"Reference group theory" pronounced by Merton is also applicable in the present study. As pointed out by Lipset and Bendix, "a fuller understanding of many varieties of social behaviour requires a knowledge of the process through which men relate themselves to groups-groups to whose values they refer their own behaviour, and with whose members they compare themselves in appraising various aspects of their situation. In explaining these processes, the term 'reference group' has been used in at least two different ways. We can utilize the convenient distinction of the comparative reference group and the normative reference group. To use a group of people as a comparative reference group is to use it as a frame of reference within which to make some judgement. To use a group as a normative reference group, on the other hand, is to take over its norms, to evulate its members. Applying the latter meaning specifically to social mobility, reference group theory suggests that the potentially upward mobile usually reveal anticipatory socialisation, that is, they absorb the norms and behaviour traits of higher strata long before they have actually changed their social position'.[19]

The men frequently orient themselves to groups other than their own in shaping their behaviour and evaluations, and it is the problems centered about this fact of orientation to non-membership groups that constituted the distinctive concern of reference group theory".[20]

"In the process of upward mobility two separate groups are simultaneously affected. First is the 'membership group' with which a particular individual is associated till the time of

19. Lipset and Bendix, *Social Mobility in Industrial Society*, University of California Press, London, 1959, pp. 256-57.
20. R.K. Merton, *Social Theory and Social Structure*, Free Press. Illinois, 1949 ; p. 336.

mobility and the second is the group (class or occupation) which he points as a consequence of mobility".[21]

The term 'relative deprivation' developed by Merton is most applicable in the case of Scheduled Castes. The concept, according to Merton, denotes the lower status of the backward classes which is characterised by disadvantages and discrimination of several kinds and of different degrees. 'Merton and Runciman put forward the notion of relative deprivation, which was made on the basis of reference group theory and social mobility by Merton (1950). Runciman (1961) worked out a typology of relative deprivation in relation to reference groups. He (1966) later developed a concept in relation to reference groups, problems of inequality and social justice. Thus, both Merton and Runciman used relative deprivation as the basis of studies of social mobility in relation to the life styles of positive reference groups".[22]

M.N. Srinivas pointed out that sanskritization has contributed much to social mobility though it did not lead to a structural change or change of the system as such. "It marked a positional change in the ranking of caste strata. The importance of sanskritisation as a process of social mobility, however, lies in the fact that it activated a series of latent structural processes within the system of stratification. Firstly, it contributed to the collective mobilisation of the aspirations of the lower castes for status ascedency, and secondly, it implied a reference model for the aspired—for status, usually of the dominant castes in the villeges or the regions concerned".[23]

21. S.M. Dubey, *Social Mobility Among Professions*, popular Prakashans, Bombay, 1975, pp. 190-91.
22. M.S.A. Rao, (1979) *op. cit.*, pp. 243-44.
23. Y.B. Damle, *Reference group theory with regard to mobility in caste*, in Silverberg (ed) Social Mobility in the caste system in India, Moutin, The Hauge, 1968, p. 68.

This kind of social mobility occurred among scheduled castes through sanskritization process. Although the change is only positional yet it has significant structural consequences, especially in relation to the orientation of the lower castes towards the traditional upper castes".[24]

Factors of Social Mobility

There are multiple factors contributing to social mobility, as pointed out by scholars such as Sorokin Cohn, Fichter, and Dubey. Sorokin has divided the factors of social mobility into primary and secondary. The primary factors are ; demographic factors dissimilarity of parents and children, change of environment, especially of the anthropo-social environmental and defective social distribution of individuals within social layers. The secondary factors discussed by Sorokin are pattern of stratification, educational opportunities, urbanization and the psycological motivations.[25]

Cohn in his study revealed that, education is the primary factor for social mobility.[26] Occupational opportunities and governmental programmes were the other factors which promote mobility among scheduled castes.

According to Joseph H. Fitcher "the person who is striving for upward mobility must have access to the objects that give high status". The conditions that help or hinner this access may be called the factors of mobility. For any particular individual who has the personal abilities as well as the desire for upward mobility, the following conditioning factors must be taken into consideration :

24. M.N. Srinivas *et.al. Dimensions of Social Change*, Allied Publishers Pvt. Ltd., Bombay, 1977, p. 141.
25. S.M. Lipset and H.L. Zatterberg, *A Theory of Social Mobility in Class, Status and Power*, edited by Lipset and Bendix, Free Press, New York, 1966, p. 346.
26. B.S. Cohn, Chamar Family in a North Indian Village, *Economic and Political Weekly*, July 1961, p. 1052.

(a) The policy and practice of immigration into a total society and into a local community will greatly affect the possibilities of upward mobility.

(b) The presence or absence of individual competition as a value in the culture significantly affects mobility. A competitive society actually encourages upward mobility, but it also permits downward mobility of unsuccessful persons.

(c) The availability of opportunities to prepare oneself for the competitive process is a secondary factor.

(d) The pattern of equality and inequality in a society have much to do with the chances of social mobility.[27]

"The revolutionary changes in the system of transportation and communication have shortened the distance of time and place, resulting in a high degree of horizontal mobility in the form of immegration, displaccment and shift from one place to another. Growth of population is another factor which is producing regional and territorial mobility"[28]

Review of Related Studies

Lipset and Bendix (1959) : Conducted an empirical study on mobility in Oakland and California. They found that the rate of social mobility was similar in all industrial societies like Sweden, Japan, Italy and Great Britain. The study also analysed in detail the political implication of mobility and explored the relationship between education and mobility. Lipset and Bendix pointed out that the direction of social mobility in American society was from mutual to non-mutual occupations. In the case of occupational mobility, the data shows that men are more likely to change from one job to another than to

27. Joseph H. Fitcher, *Sociology*, the University of Chicago Press, London, 1971.

28. S.M. Dubey (1975) *Op. cit.*, pp. 16-17.

shift occupations. His study concludes that spread of technical education and the improvement of general education have greatly stimulated the vertical mobility of the population.

Vagiswari (1973) : Studied 800 Harijan households and 197 non-harijan households from ten villages of Tamil Nadu. The results showed that there still existed a great deal of latent and over discrimination against Harijans; but when constrasted with the discrimination embodied in social and religious belief of the war past, the trend towards social equality is definite though very slow moving.

Social mobility among Professions in Gorakhpur ; a study conducted by S.M. Dubey (1975) is based on three generations of the members of six professions viz. Civil and railway officials, college teachers, medical doctors, engineers, lawyers and University teachers. Data collection was based on both interview schedule and participant observation. The sample size was 300, among them 269 were males and 31 were females. The study also analysed intergenerational occupational mobility. The study revealed that the respondents of Gorakhpur engaged in caste occupations—agricultural labour, cultivation, landlordship, business and clerical jobs—has considerably declined in the generation of father. Among the college teachers too, the percentage of caste occupations have declined in the generation of the father. The same trend was seen in the case of Engineers, Doctors, Lawyers and Legal Medical professions. Comparative study of different professions revealed that no occupational change has taken place among doctors and engineers, because of the nature of their education. People belonging to lower occupations have improved their lot by joining different professions and no case of downward mobility was found among intra-generation.

Harshad R. Trivedi (1976) : Studied the 'Exploitation of Scheduled Caste Women', in three districts of the Punjab state. 203 respondents of harijan women were selected randomly, and information collected through interview schedule. A few case studies were also conducted. The findings are changed in various aspects of life including values, attitudes, patterns of behaviour, physical and social mobility, etc., among scheduled castes is generally initiated by men and not by the women of the community. There was a greater tendency among young wives of educated and urban based husbands to establish nuclear families in order to gain greater freedom of action, and to improve their status. On account of lack of literacy, most of the scheduled caste women continued to do the same type of low paid labourious occupations and were not able to migrate to urban areas, temporarily or permanently, without the help of men some of whom are reported to have inducted them into immoral traffic. The status of selected scheduled caste women in matters of adopting dress, ornament, dietary habits, etc. from the high castes, without any inhibitions has been greatly improved but is restricted to those coming from educated families or those living in urban areas. Inter-caste marriages of scheduled caste women with high caste men were not numerous. The conventional marriage ceremonies are not only being sanskritized, but the practice of bride-price, too, is being replaced by dowry, indicating a tendency of evaluating the status to marriageable girls in the light of values of high caste Hindu society.

L. P. Vidyarthi's (*1977*) : Work which gives a comparative account of the life and culture of the Scheduled Castes was based on field work done in two major cultural and linguistic zones of Bihar. The main findings of the study were the following. Owing to the factors of industrialisation, urbanization, westernization, growth in the modern means of communication, impact of democracy and social-legislation, the caste-system in general is weakening. Despite the legislation to declare the untouchability as an offence, the age old system of untouchability is still persistent. The scheduled castes of tribal zone worship mostly natural objects like sun God, great mountains, watergod etc. They worship ancestoral spirits and hunting spirits. They believed in the concepts of salvation, soul and rebirth. Old names of scheduled castes are being replaced by the new sanskritized ones. The scheduled castes of Magahi zone are also trying hard to raise their social status by Sanskritizing themselves. Majority of them were following (traditional) agricultural operations such as transplantation harvesting and weeding.

C. Rajagopalan (1978) : Studied social mobility among the scheduled castes of Bangalore city, in 76 village and 34 towns among 3338 families. The study was mainly aimed at ascertaining the extent and magnitude of change which has taken place in the conditions of scheduled castes.

The findings of the study revealed that education influences mobility in occupational status between respondent's fathers and respondent's generation. Another fact was that the respondent's occupation is significant in determining his son's educational mobility. The intergenerational mobility of respondents in educational and occupational status showed that respondent's education and occupation had causal relationship with his son's generations. Higher the level of education, greater is the rate of occupational mobility among the respondents.

It was also revealed that the occupation of a vast industry in certain large centres, the village tanners enterprise is being reduced to smaller dimension. Chamars of that district have a reputation for witchcraft and this is borne out by abundant practice both of white and black magic, while the domestic ceremonies of the chamars show much Brahminical influence.

Suneila Malik (1979): Conducted a study on "social integration of scheduled castes" in Ambala city. 295 cases were selected for the study. Findings showed that the scheduled castes have been improving their-socio-economic status in terms of education, occupation and income. The study also revealed that education is an index of socio-economic status along which social mobility has been measured. The measurement of social mobility in three generations was done with the comparison of educational and occupational status of the respondents with those of their fathers and grand-fathers. Results showed that higher the status of the father, the smaller proportion of sons in the lower occupational grades, and lower the status of the father, the smaller the proportion of sons in the higher occupational grades. This in turn showed that occupational prestige grade of the father affected the occupational prestige grade of the son. The same trend was seen in the case of educational mobility. The higher the education of the father, the higher was the education of the son. The study also revealed that social status of an individual is influenced not merely by his individual possessions, but also by the social status of the group to which he belongs. In order to raise their social status, the scheduled castes are adopting the way of life of the higher castes. The study concluded that a small minority of scheduled castes were upwardly mobile, who have attained higher standards of education and are occupying high posts. They are becoming modernized and are following the pattern of living of the higher castes in all respects.

Mumtaz Ali Khan (*1980*): Examined the changes, which have taken place in several aspects of the life of the scheduled castes in Karnataka The study also assessed the impact of various measures adopted for the welfare of the scheduled castes. The sample size was 500 and data collection done through interview schedule. The study showed that adult males have a higher percentage of literacy than the female respondents. Nearly three-fourth of the respondents favour boy's education and girl's education for knowledge, indicating thereby that the respondents are aware of the value of education for the progress of their boys ane girls. The main reason for illiteracy among the respondents were economic handicap, domestic problems, inadequacy or absence of Governmental assistance etc.

The study of inter-generational mobility pointed out that the highest peicentage of deviation from father's occupation was in the case of cultivation followed by unskilled labour. Majority of the respondents were unskilled or some skilled variety and many of them were still in the traditional occupation. Respondent's occupation was influenced by the father's occupation. In all occupational categories the highest percentage of respondents were in the same occupation as their father's. Traditional occupations were still concentrated among respondents in the old age group. Non-traditional occupations of low status are mostly followed by the respondents in the middle age group and the non-traditional occupations of higher status were mostly in the hands of the younger age group. In terms of status categories, rate of upward mobility was higher in lower status than in the medium status. Much of it only moved up to medium status, very few had moved from low to high status category.

Savitha Mehra (1982): Studied "Social mobility in Rural Haryana". The study made it clear that educated respondents have enhanced their occupational status through education by shifting towards urban occupation. The study concluded that higher the education of the respondents, higher was their father's and grand father's education, and lower the education of the respondent, lower was their father's and grand father's education. The advanced regions provide more occupational opportunities to the respondents in enhancing their occupational status.

Inter-and Intra-generational occupational mobility showed that persons were occupationally mobile in two ways ; firstly they adopt the occupation which exists in the village itself, secondly, they turn to urban market for getting better employment. The study also pointed out that the high occupational mobility among untouchables may be due to various governmental welfare measures and special job provisions.

M. Showeb (1986) examined the socio-economic changes of chamar community in the Varanasi district of Uttar Pradesh. In order to measure the social changes taking place among them, the study adopted a comparative framework. The sample size consisted of 150 respondents, 50 cases from each category. On the oneside the Chamars engaged in traditional occupations, on the other side, the educated chamars engaged in modern salaried occupations; who through education, job reservation and other measures of economic betterment, have achieved a new socio-economic status which delinks them from their traditional social nexus. There was also a third category of respondents who were students of Chamar Community.

The educational profile of the respondent's families showed that proportion of illiterate members has been found higher among the traditlonal employed respondents. Younger generation of Chamars was becoming more inclined to formal education. It was also found that low academic achievement may be a function of their low economic background. The analysis of career mobility of respondents showed that a number of respondents have shifted from one job position to other and have also got promotion in the work organizations in which they are currently engaged. As regards the manner of recruitment, 70 per cent of employed respondents have been selected under the reserved quota. The study also pointed out that in the interaction between traditional and educated Chamars, the educated often ignored and kept distance with traditional Chambers. Their attitude towards the settlement of marriage, faith in the doctrine of Karma, religious beliefs, worshiping pattern etc. were also undergoing change. The study concluded that education, modern occupation, and the welfare schemes of the Government are contributing a lot towards changing the socio-cultural attitude and life style of the Chamar Community.

C. Parvathamma and Satyanarayana (*1984*): Conducted a study on "New horizons and scheduled castes" in Karnataka city. The study concentrated on the educational problems and other difficulties at Scheduled Caste college students in Karnataka. The sample size was 260 scheduled caste college students.

The study revealed that the progress of education among scheduled castes is very slow in the state. Inspite of incentives provided, there were only few students from these communities in institutions of higher education. There was large scale wastage and stagnation in education in these communities. The education of the parents and siblings of the students in the study is very poor, almost nil.

Most of the students know the constitutional provisions regarding reservation of jobs and seats to communities.

Even though many have stated that they have not experienced any discrimination because they are Scheduled Castes, for some, it is the worst experience. A large number of such discriminations were problems connected with untouchability.

Soran Singh (1987) studied about the changing socio-economic conditions of the scheduled castes with special reference to district Jaunpur in eastern Uttar Pradesh. The sample size was 400 Scheduled Caste respondents. The findings of the study broadly point out the position of the scheduled castes in social hierarchy has considerably improved. Similarly, there was change in areas like social contact, proximity and social outlook, occupation, economic condition, education, health and sanitation, and housing. Among the respondents, aspiration for children's jobs is quite high and points to an urge for social climbing.

Ramashray Roy and V.B. Singh (1987) conducted a study in Uttar Pradesh to assess the views of Scheduled Caste elites on matters concerning their own community vis-a-vis the society at large. The sample was 55 individual cases, and the data was collected through interview schedule. They explored the educational background of respondent's father and grand father in order to ascertain the kind of educational environment in the family, and was found that there was a depressing picture about the educational attainment of the respondent's two earlier generations. In sharp contrast to the generations of their fathers and grand fathers, only 7 of the respondents discontinued their education beyond high school, and all the rest have sudied beyond college level. In the case of occupational structure, there was upward mobility reflecting an improvement. There was a good deal of occupational differentiation in the case of fathers as against the grand fathers. In the case of third generation, the respondents of the study found further differentiation in the occupational structure viewed in this perspective, occupational mobility was undoubtedly very remarkable.

They also examined the phenomenon of social mobility of the elites to explore their friendship circle. The achievements made by elites in this study, in the area of education and occupation have been instrumental in enhancing the chances of their social acceptability.

As they move to higher age groups, very few females had the opportunity to avail education. Atrocities on the scheduled castes and their exploitation are often associated with rural society, and the most important problem that the elites perceived to be confronting the untouchables are poverty and untouchability.

K. Saradamoni (1981) conducted a study in Trivandrum district in Kerala. The four types of respondents selected for the study were pulayas, other scheduled castes, other backward communities, and forward castes. The sample size was 336 cases and the data collected through interview schedule.

The study revealed that, to a large extent, social mobility has taken place in the study area. Demands of development, urbanisation, new occupational roles, and positions of leadership have created new opportunities for individual achievement and mobility. In this study among the scheduled castes, the majority of whom were agrestic slaves, did not use land as a means towards upward mobility. The political struggles and social reforms movements which gave impetus to Harijan agitations had stressed the importance of land reforms in social change.

The findings again showed that women, on the whole, have suffered more out of the ill patterned development in the post-independent decades. The period when initial mobility took place did not witness an independent women's movement. The Pulaya women have been able to make use of the limited opportunities, more than the other scheduled castes.

Shantha Kumari (N.D) examined the impact of welfare measures among scheduled castes in Kerala.

The study revealed that welfare programmes have benefited the scheduled castes to some extent though they have not been able to make as much impact on them as was envisaged in these programmes.

Though the rate of mobility between two generations in this study was high, vertical occupational mobility among them was quite negligible. In her sample, job reservation do not have helped the scheduled castes significantly. Training in traditional crafts and occupations has not made any impact in providing occupational mobility. Scheduled Castes were of the view that the training in traditional occupations only perpetuates their traditional status.

Education has gone a long way in the transformation of traditional beliefs and customs. Social barriers imposed by the high caste have been chiefly responsible for preventing the full utilization of Government welfare programmes by the scheduled castes.

There was improvement in the educational progress of the scheduled castes after the introduction of special educational concessions to them. The study also revealed that financial concession in education had contributed to lessening of the burden of education to the scheduled castes. It was also found that education was a factor for better mingling with higher castes. It is clearly pronounced in the study that the scheduled castes realised the potential of education to bring about social and occupational mobility.

P. Nirmala Bhai (1986) examined the status mobility of Harijan women of Kerala.

The findings of the study pointed out that Harijan women in Kerala have been improving their general socio-economic status along the dimensions of education, occupation, and income. The study confirmed the fact that the educational aspirations among the Harijan women and their family members enabled them to improve their status in society. Welfare measures contributed to the improvement of education and hence to elevate the status of Harijan women. From this study, it was obvious that parent's interest in elevating status of their children is very high among Harijans in Kerala. Harijan women as a whole are desirous of getting one or other kind of employment and through this they aspire to improve their position in the society. The study further revealed that Harijan women of Kerala exhibited an inverse relationship between level of education and political participation. Majority of Harijan women preferred endogamous type of marriage to intercaste marriage. The Harijan women in Kerala have a special drive for possessing new traits of achieved status through adoptions of new or modifications of existing customs.

The review of these studies shows that though both in India and in Kerala many studies have been conducted on different aspects of mobility among Scheduled Castes. Social mobility of Scheduled Caste women remains comparatively an unexplored area. There are gaps in our knowledge about social mobility in areas like education, inter-generational occupation, intragenerational occupation, customs, beliefs and aspirations of Scheduled Caste women in Kerala. The present study is an attempt to investigate the rate, areas and factors of social mobility among the Scheduled Caste women in Kerala. For a comprehensive understanding of the pattern of social mobility, two generations have been studied.

CHAPTER II

Methodology

The Problem

In the traditional Indian society, social stratification was based on the caste system, according to which, a person's status was determined by his birth. The system further constitutes a status hierarchy with the Brahmins at the top and the scheduled castes at the bottom. As a result, the scheduled castes are characterised by the lowest social status in the caste hierarchy. They were subjected to a number of disabilities and disadvantages as a consequence of their low socio-economic status. Besides, they were segregated from the mainstream of the society. These castes in the past had no access to educa-cation. Scheduled Caste women all over India had several handicaps for leading a normal social life. Traditionally, they were engaged in menial occupations such as agriculture work, tatooing, collecting, firewoods from forest etc., and accordingly their social position has been very low.

According to 1981 Census, the Scheduled Castes constituted 15.28 per cent of the nation's population, and among them 48.25 per cent were females. In the case of Kerala, 10.04 per cent of the state's population are scheduled castes and 50.54 per cent of them are females. For centuries, scheduled castes are economically, educationally and socially depressed groups. The Government of India and State Governments are very anxious to uplift the lower castes by improving the conditions of scheduled castes in order to bring them the mainstream of the society. Accordingly, there were many Acts and policies to help them.

Since the introduction of the Constitution, a deliberate attempt had been going on in India from the part of the Governmental machinery to improve the social life of the Harijans through several programmes. Numerous facilities have been provided to the scheduled castes with a view to enable them to take their rightful place in society. Through Five Year Plans, the Government have made targets for the improvement of social conditions of scheduled castes in general and scheduled castes women in particular. Consequently, the position of the scheduled caste women had changed and there is noticeable improvement in many areas such as education, occupation and other socio-cultural fields. The process of social mobility is the result of many factors, the important among them being social stratification, size of the community, modernisation, education, technology and economy.

In the case of Kerala state, the major factors which contribute to the social mobility of scheduled castes in general and their women in particular, are improvement in educational level, opportunities for modern occupation, widening of inter-caste relations, development of modern attitude towards social issues etc.

Literature such as census reports, reports of the Commissioner of Scheduled Castes and Scheduled Tribes, Planning Commission reports, provide some yardsticks for measuring changes as far as the demographic and educational fields are concerned. But no systematic and scientific effort has been made so far to find out the factors responsible and rate of social mobility among the scheduled caste women in Kerala. Therefore, the present investigation is intended to assess social mobility by comparing, occupational, economic and educational background, level of aspiration, attitudes on and practice of different social issues, of two generations of scheduled caste women daughters and their mothers. Such a study may be quite useful in increasing our present knowledge of this community and in giving useful information to the planners and policy makers engaged in the uplift of scheduled caste women.

2. Objectives

(1) To find out whether there is social mobility among the scheduled caste women.

(2) if there is mobility, to identify, the factors responsible for it.

(3) to assess the areas where mobility is clearly pronounced.

(4) and finally, if there is no mobility, to find out the factors responsible for it.

3. Hypotheses

Our main hypothesis is that there is social mobility among scheduled caste women, and education has contributed to the social mobility. The sub-hypothesis are :

(a) There is considerable educational mobility within the two generations of scheduled castes women.

(b) Intergenerational occupational mobility is vertical among scheduled caste women, though intra-generational occupational mobility is horizontal.

(c) Inferiority feelings still prevalent among the Scheduled Caste women prevent their educational attainment and consequently contribute to their low rate of occupational mobility.

(d) Occupational improvement contributes to the social status of scheduled caste women, and

(e) There is greater mobility in the attitudes and reactions of scheduled caste women towards many common social issues.

4. Definition of Key Concepts

Social mobility has been defined by various scholars. The term according to Paul B. Horton refers to the "act of moving from one social status to another".[1]

Auguste Comte was of the opinion that "social mobility is the part of the broader concept of social change".[2]

S.M. Lipset and R. Bendix defined the concept as "the process by which individuals move from one position to another in society—positions which by general consent have been given specific hierarchical values".[3]

According to P.A. Sorokin "when an individual or a phenomenon passes from one stage to the other, it is termed as "Social mobility". In his words, social mobility is "any transition of an individual or social object or value nothing that has been created of what arrived by human activity from one social position to another."[4]

In the present study, social mobility refers to the transition of two generations of scheduled caste women from one position to another.

1. Horton, B. Paul, "*Sociology*" McGraw Hill Kogakusha Ltd. Tokyo, 1976, p. 269.
2. S.M. Miller, "*Comparative Social Mobility*", A Trend Report and Bibliography. Current Sociology, Vol. IX, No. 1, Basil Black Well, 1969.
3. S.M. Lipset and R. Bendix, *Op. cit.*, pp. 1-2.
4. P.A. Sorokin, "*Contemporary Sociological Theories*", Harper and Row Publishers, New York, 1964, p. 749.

Scheduled Caste Women

"The term "scheduled castes" consist of those castes which are included in a Schedule of the Constitution of India. The term "scheduled castes" read by Article 341 of the Constitution as "the President may with respect to any state and where it is specified in Part A or Part B of the first schedule, after consultation with the Governor or Raj Pramukh thereof, by public notification, specify the castes, races or tribes which shall be deemed to be scheduled castes for the purpose of the Constitution".[5] Female members of the scheduled caste community is studied here under the title of scheduled caste women.

5. Population and Sample

The population for the study constitutes the scheduled caste women of Kerala. Though they are spread over the entire length and breath of the state, there are certain districts which have larger concentration of scheduled castes than others. Thus, three districts of Kerala, viz., Palghat, Alleppey and Trivandrum were selected for drawing sample for the study. The districts were selected because, according to the population rates of the scheduled castes, Palghat occupies first position (14.77%) and Trivandrum the fourth position (11.11%) and Alleppy the fifth position (9.23%). Education is a major vehicle for social mobility and hence educationally backward areas and forward areas were taken for measuring social mobility. Palghat is educationally backward area, with the literacy rate of 58 per cent. At the same time, Alleppy (the literacy is 78.52 per cent) and Trivandrum (70 50%) are educationally forward. Based on the 1981 Census data, representative taluks were selected from each of these districts on the basis of high concentration of Scheduled Castes. Ottappalam (22.26%), Alathur (20.38%) and Chittoor (16.24%) taluks were selected

5. Basu Durga Das, "*Commentary on the Constitution of India*" Sarkar and Sons Ltd., Calcutta, 1956, p. 530.

from Palghat. Chengannur North (16.32%), Mavelikkara (15.84%) and Thiruvalla (10.66%) taluks were selected from Alleppey. Finally, from Trivandrum, Chirayinkil (15.37%), Trivandrum (10.36%) and Nedumangad (9.76%) taluks were selected. Since the majority of the scheduled castes are located in the rural areas, our study concentrated on rural scheduled caste population. However, in the case of Trivandrum district, the respondents belonged to urban areas as well.

The Panchayat register of households and the electoral rolls do not mention community and as there is no agency which maintains community-wise lists of all the people, the investigator found it very difficult to locate the scheduled caste households. We, therefore, approached the District Harijan Welfare Officer to get some clue to the distribution of the scheduled castes in the district. He could give us the names of villages in which scheduled castes were concentrated. We got the addresses of scheduled caste households from the block officers, which they had selected for welfare work. The scheduled caste leaders also helped us to identify the scheduled caste households. This facilitated our task to some extent.

In order to assess the rate and areas of social mobility, 450 scheduled caste women of two generations were chosen. Of the total respondents, 225 were mothers and 225 were their daughters having 18 and above years. Stratified random samping method was used to select the sample. The researcher made household visits to identify the mothers 18 and above years old daughters. The sample was then stratified on the basis of the daughter's age. The justification for the selection of 18 and above years old daughter was that the Untouchability Offence Act was implemented in 1955, and the mother of the 18 years old daughter might have suffered the hardships from the practice of untouchability. At the same time, for the daughters who were born after 1955, the situation is entirely different.

Another reason was that the National policy on education was introduced in 1968, which was intended to equalise educational opportunity among scheduled castes. So, the daughter respondents might have utilised the educational facilities introduced through the national policy. Finally, the respondents below 18 may not understand and respond clearly to our questions.

6. Types of Data Collected

Three types of data were collected for the study.

(1) Documentary evidence, mainly from published materials, government reports, Census reports.

(2) Interview data from two generations of scheduled caste women.

(3) Field notes by the researcher through observation, and discussions with elder scheduled caste leaders, and local educated Harijans.

7. Tools of Data Collection

Data for the empirical study was collected mainly through interview schedules. Two separate schedules were prepared for scheduled caste women of two generations. The schedule elicited information on mobility in family and marriage, education, occupation social and cultural sphere, political participation, caste status, religious practices, and change in the way of dressing. Most of the questions were pre-coded for easy tabulation and analysis. The interview schedule consisted mostly of closed questions and only very few were open ended.

8. Pilot Study and Pre-test

With the intention of foreseeing flaws and handicaps and the plausibility of the research, a pilot study was conducted in Chirayinkil taluk of Trivandrum district and the investigator held discussions with scheduled caste leaders and elder members of the community. It has helped to a great extent in under standing the situation and problems among them, and also it proved that the study is plausible. Sixty scheduled caste women, consisting of 30 mothers and 30 daughters, were interviewed, with the help of two separate interview schedules. The interview schedule was administered to find out whether the questions were simple enough for them, and whether the data collected through them were adequate, reliable and valid. It was found that some of the questions were not understood by the respondents, mainly among elder generation and some others were repetitions. In the light of pilot study, the hypotheses were modified and finalised.

9. Pretest

Pretesting the tools of data collection before they are used in the study proper, ensures against difficulties of comprehension, ambiguities and sterility of questions. In the present study, a pretest were conducted at Kariyam in Trivandrum district, by administering the schedule to 40 scheduled caste women of two generations. The unreliable ambiguos, suggestive, and repetitive questions were suitably modified or discarded. The questions were then coded.

10. Data Collection

The field study, relating to this study was conducted from January to July, 1986. The researcher stayed in each district for two to three months. Being a stranger to the place, establishing rapport with the respondents found to be very difficult, in the beginning. In Palghat, all the respondents of elder generations being illiterate and having little exposure to the wider community, it was very difficult to make them understand the purpose of visit. Scattered households posed more difficult problems. Some settlements and Harijan colonies were situated in the interior of villages. In those cases, transportation was also a problem. The investigator had to walk several kilometres to locate the houses. One main difficulty was that between 10 a.m. and 5 p.m. one could find no grown-up member in the family as all of them would have gone out for work. In such cases, early or late visits were the only solution. Another problem was to find out both mothers and their daughters. In some cases daughters were living far away from mother's house.

Some respondents mistook the researcher for a government official from scheduled caste department. Some others took her for an official for giving agriculture pension, old age pension, etc. In some places, people asked the purpose of interviewing adult girls. However, when the researcher could convince them of the purpose, they did co-operate fully. When promised not to disclose their identity, they were ready to provide us with information. Another problem faced by the researcher was with the language. Though all the respondents spoke Malayalam, the state language, they used different pronounciations, words and accent. This was more in Palghat district where the literacy rate was the lowest among scheduled castes. In the case of Alleppey, such problems were comparatively less. This may be because of the higher level of literacy in this district. However, these difficulties were over after the first few days of field work. Usually, the interview lasted for 50 to 60 minutes depending on the time required to establish rapport.

11. **Analysis of Data**

The data collected were tabulated manually. Statistical tests like Chi-square and correlations were applied in most cases. In a few cases, the data clearly indicate the trend, and as such, no statistical correlations have been worked out. In some cases Chi-square test and contingency coefficient of correlation have been calculated to facilitate comparison. These calculations were done on the basis of the variables like age, income, education, occupation, caste, and place of birth.

12. Case Study

In addition to the empirical data collected, two 'cases' were selected from Kariyam and Venganoor in Trivandrum district. The objective of the case studies was to gain in-depth knowledge about various aspects of social mobility among the scheduled caste women and to illustrate the findings of the empirical study.

CHAPTER III

Educational Mobility

The Scheduled Castes, most of which had been subjected to various social disabilities of extreme nature were exploited and kept subservient mainly because they were illiterates. Their mass illiteracy was, in turn, due to religious and social sanctions imposed on them by caste Hindus. Education is a dynamic agent of social change and social mobility. Education has a major role in enabling a person to acquire modern occupation leading to higher economic status, and thus social mobility. "The role of education as a catalyst or agent of social change has been well recognized. Education is said to determine the level of aspiration, technology, productivity, efficiency etc., which constitute some of the basic factors in the process of development."[1]

Oommen has argued in favour of "education' being the

34. N.J. Usha Rao, *Women in a Developing Society*, Asia Publishing House, New Delhi, 1983, p. 27.

strategic point for initiating social change. According to him it enables members of the society to play new roles.[2]

The significance of formal education in social mobility had been pointed out by M.S.A. Rao. "Education helps in promoting values and achieving new goals. It is widely recognised that formal education plays a vital role in social mobility, both horizontal and vertical. If formal education is seen as a socialising agency preparing individuals for a style of life associated with a stratum, it is at the same time an agency helping individuals to overcome prejudices, and promoting values and behaviour of a more universalistic nature."[3]

Both the Government of India and the State, have been convinced of the crucial role of education and have placed great emphasis on it so as to improve the conditions of the scheduled castes. Accordingly, they have used education as the prime mover in the welfare policies and programmes intended for the scheduled castes. This is reflected in the special concessions and facilities being provided for the education of the scheduled castes.

Scheduled Castes and Education

Lannoy observes that "the greatest source of hope to Harijans is modern education which acts as a solvent of caste barriers".[4]

Kerala is considered to be the most progressive among the Indian States with the highest rate of literacy. Literacy is an important demographic characterstic which is a pointer to the

2. T.K. Oommen, "Strategy for social change", A study on Untouchability", *Economic and Political Weekly*, Vol. III No. 25, June 1968, pp. 933-936.
3. M.S.A. Rao, *Tradition, Rationality and Change*, Popular Prakashan, Bombay, 1972, pp. 131-132.
4. Richard Lannoy, *The Speaking Tree*, Oxford University Press, London, 1971, p. 254.

level of advancement of the people. It is all the more significant in the case of scheduled castes and scheduled tribes, since most of them were confined to darkness of illiteracy and ignorance for centuries.

It is true that literacy rate of Harijans in Kerala is higher than the national average. Literacy rate among scheduled castes is lower when compared to that of non-scheduled castes in various regions of India. This is mainly because they have been prohibited from learning since ages. However, in recent times, particularly after independence, their literacy rate has been improving. Their literacy level is around one per cent both in rural and urban areas in all the states in India, except in Kerala where it is around 2 per cent.

Scheduled Caste Women and Education

From the beginning of this century, it was realised that the spread of education amongst women was the only means through which status improvement is possible. Hence, education has been identified as an important factor in women's emancipation.

"The emphasis on female education was accepted as an element of state policy by the princely rulers of Kerala. So much so that when independence came, Kerala was leading India not only in general literacy, but in female literacy also".[5]

The literacy rate of females belonging to scheduled castes is very low in India. The reason for this is, scheduled caste population is socially backward, and oppressed, and among them the position of female is the worst.

The study "Education and Social Change" by Narendra K. Singhi revealed that "the literacy rate among scheduled caste

5. P.K.B. Nayar, 'Family as a Determinant of Women's Social Status' *Kerala Sociologist*, Vol. XIII, No. 2, July-December 1985, p. 8.

males is considerably higher compared to that of their women folk. "The scheduled caste females thus suffer double deprivation. First, they belong to a backward caste and second, they are deprived of basic opportunities of life being born girls which implies inherent social inequality based on sex'.[6]

During recent years, Kerala has shown a higher literacy rate of scheduled castes than the other states of India.

Factors Influencing Education

Education is said to the usher some changes in the life pattern of people and it has been treated as an index for measuring social mobility. There are some variables which influence the level of education of an individual, like age, caste, place of birth, and income.

Age

Age always remains an important factor influencing the education of an individual. The younger generation, having better opportunities and being more conscious about the value of education is usually better educated than those belonging to the elder generation.

Our study, also indicates age as an important factor influencing education. Age of the respondents and their level of education are significantly related to each other, i.e., as age increases, the level of education decreares. Table no. 5 makes it clear.

The table reveals that none of the respondents who belonged to the age group below 20 was illiterate, 58.82 per cent of the independents belonging to the above 50 age group illiterate and none of them had college education. This may be because in older days women's education was not common. They were not aware of the educational facilities and their advantage in life. Elder generation of scheduled caste women

6. Narendra K. Singhi, *Education and Social Change*, Rawat Publications, Jaipur, 1979, p. 27.

TABLE 5

Daughters' Age and Level of Education

Daughters' Age	Level of Education						
	Illiterate	Primary	Upper Primary	High School	SSLC	College	Total
Below 20	0	1 1.75%	9 15.79%	18 31.58%	19 33.33%	10 17.54%	57 26.33%
20—29	3 3.95%	5 6.58%	9 11.84%	22 28.95%	25 32.89%	12 15.79%	76 33.78%
30—39	5 11.11%	4 8.89%	6 13.33%	12 26.67%	16 35.56%	2 4.44%	45 20.00%
40—49	8 26.67%	2 6.67%	4 13.33%	5 16.67%	10 33.33%	1 3.33%	30 13.33%
50+	10 58.82%	1 5.88%	2 11.77%	3 17.65%	1 5.88%	0	17 7.56%
Total	26 11.56%	13 5.78%	30 13.33%	60 26.67%	71 31.55%	25 11.11%	225

never got the chance to attend schools, owing to many reasons. But today parents are more ambitious about the future of their children and, therefore, pay more attention to the education of their children. So children of the younger age groups are having higher education.

The same trend could be seen in the case of mother respondents. It is noticed that there is a sudden fall in the illiteracy rate in the older generation between the age groups 40-49 and 50-59. It may be stated that this is the group which benefited from government's welfare measures since independence, which may be due to special component education plans given to scheduled castes by the Government.

Caste

Though all the scheduled castes are educationally backward, there is variation in the level of education among the different caste groups in our study. The data relating to these are presented in Table no 6. It was evident that of all castes, Kannakkans, Cheramar, and Cherumans were the most educationally backward. Sambavas and Thandans had relatively higher educational level, because none of them was illiterate. 44.44 per cent of Thandans had high school education and college education. Thandans seemed to be more educated because their children did not have to help their parents in traditional work like 'coconut palm plaiting' a difficult process for children. In the case of other Scheduled Caste children, they had to help their parents in work such as agriculture. Thus higher education came to be plausible for them.

In the case of mother respondents also the same trend was seen ie., Thandan mothers respondents were educated than that of other castes. Kanakkans and Cheruman respondents belonged to Palghat district. Palghat was the most educationally backward area in the state. Another reason for illiteracy among these people was lack of awareness about the advantages of education, and consequently female education was not given priority, and dropouts among girls were common.

TABLE 6

Daughters' caste and level of education.

Daughter's Caste	Level of Education						
	Illiterate	Primary	Upper Primary	High School	SSLC	College	Total
1	2	3	4	5	6	7	8
Pulaya	3 4.00%	1 1.33%	14 18.67%	22 29.33%	25 33.33%	10 13.33%	75 33.33%
Kurava	1 2.78%	0	10 27.78%	2 5.56%	21 58.33%	2 5.55%	36 16.00%
Mannan	0	0	3 21.43%	4 28.57%	1 7.14%	6 42.86%	14 6.22%
Vedar	1 11.11%	0	0	6 66.67%	2 22.22%	0	9 4.00%
Sambava	0	0	0	2 50.00%	2 50.00%	0	4 1.77%

(Contd.)

1	2	3	4	5	6	7	8
Thandar	0	0	0	4 44.44%	1 11.11%	4 44.44%	9 4.00%
Cheramar	2 25.00%	3 37.05%	0	0	1 12.50%	2 25.00%	8 3.55%
Kanakkan	7 43.75%	6 37.50%	2 12.50%	0	0	1 6.25%	16 29.63%
Cherumar	12 22.22%	3 5.56%	1 1.85%	20 37.04%	18 33.33%	0	54 24.00%
Total	26 11.55%	13 5.78%	30 13.33%	60 26.67%	71 31.56%	25 11.11%	225

Place of Residence

Level of education of the respondents varied in accordance with the districts to which they belonged Alleppey had the highest level of literacy (78.52%) followed by Trivandrum (70.50%) and Palghat is the most backward (58%). The same trend is visible among our respondents which is given in table No. 7.

6.67 per cent of respondents belonging to Trivandrum and and 28 per cent of respondents belonging to Palghat were illiterate. At the same time, not a single respondent from Alleppey was illiterate. In the case of higher education, the same trend was seen. The most highly educated respondents were from Alleppey (16%) and Trivandrum (13.33%). It may be assumed that educationally forward area had educated people and they were aware of the need of education and they paid more attention to their children's studies.

The above table shows that 41.33 per cent of the mother respondents in Trivandrum, and 49.33 per cent in Alleppey were illiterate. It is interesting to note that cent per cent of the mother respondents belonging to Palghat were illiterate.

Income

"Income is one of the major factors in the economic conditions of the people, especially among the Scheduled Castes. Being the most backward class in the country and having been denied the right to own property, they entirely depended upon the income from their employment. Since employment opportunities in the past were strictly governed by caste status, it was not possible for Scheduled Castes to increase their income in the absence of a major change."[7]

An attempt has been made to study the economic status and educational level of the respondents.

7. Mumtaz Ali Khan Scheduled Castes and Status in India, Uppal Publishing House, New Delhi, 1980, p. 101.

TABLE 7

Daughters' Place of Birth and Educational Level.

Place of birth	*Level of Education*						
	Illiterate	*Primary*	*Upper Primary*	*High School*	*SSLC*	*College*	*Total*
Alleppey	0	1	8	20	34	12	75
		1.33%	10.67%	26.66%	45.33%	16.00%	33.33%
Trivandrum	5	3	8	24	25	10	75
	6.67%	4.00%	10.67%	32.00%	33.33%	13.33%	33.33%
Palghat	21	9	14	16	12	3	75
	28.00%	12.00%	18.67%	21.33%	16.00%	4.00%	33.33%
Total	26	13	30	60	71	25	225
	11.56%	5.78%	13.33%	26.66%	31.56%	11.11%	

TABLE 8

Mothers' Place of Birth and Educational Level

Place of birth	Mother's Education						
	Illiterate	Primary	Upper Primary	High School	SSLC	College	Total
Trivandrum	31 41.33%	30 40.00%	5 8.00%	4 5.33%	2 2.67%	2 2.67%	75 33.33%
Alleppey	37 49.33%	23 30.67%	11 14.67%	2 2.67%	2 2.67%	0	75 33.33%
Palghat	75 100.00%	0	0	0	0	0	75 33.33%
Total	143 63.56%	53 23.56%	17 7.56%	6 2.67%	4 1.78%	2 0.89%	225

TABLE 9

Parents' Income and Daughters' Level of Education.

Level of Education	Parent's Income (In Rs.)								
	Below 100	*101-200*	*201-300*	*301-400*	*401-500*	*501-600*	*601-700*	*701 and Above*	*Total*
1	2	3	4	5	6	7	8	9	10
Illiterate	14 53.84%	9 34.62%	3 11.54%	0	0	0	0	0	26 11.55%
Primary	6 46.15%	6 46.15%	1 7.69%	0	0	0	0	0	13 5.78%
Upper Primary	4 13.33%	11 36.67%	3 10.00%	6 20.00%	4 13.33%	2 6.67%	0	0	30 13.33%
High School	4 6.66%	36 60.00%	13 21.67%	4 6.67%	0	2 3.33%	1 1.67%	0	60 26.67%

S.S.L.C.	0	40 56.34%	11 15.49%	4 5.63%	2 2.88%	1 1.41%	8 11.27%	5 7.04%	71 31.56%
College	0	5 20.00%	10 40.00%	2 8.00%	2 8.00%	1 4.00%	0	5 20.00%	25 11.11%
Total	28 12.44%	107 47.56%	41 18.22%	16 7.11%	8 3.56%	6 2.67%	9 4.00%	10 4.00%	225

Table 9 shows that 53.85 per cent of the repondents belonging to the income group below Rs. 100 were illiterate. In this income group none of them had college education. On the other hand, those among income group Rs. 601-700 and above Rs. 700, not even a single respondent was illiterate, 20 per cent of them was college educated. Thus we can infer from this table that as income of parents increased education of their children also increased. It may be noted that high income group parents were having higher education and occupation and because they were aware of the advantages of education, can take more interest in the education of their children. They can also afford the expenses for children's education. In brief, high income group parents were able to provide a suitable atmosphere for their children's education.

Reasons for Illiteracy

In India, education of untouchables was considered as an offence by certain sections of society. As a result, they were denied educational opportunities and had remained illiterate.

Parvathamma states that "education has not reached the bulk or Scheduled Castes, staying in villages because of poverty, ignorence and lack of knowledge about existing facilities, absence compulsory education in primary and secondary levels and the traditional apathy for education on account of social and environmental conditions and occupational handicaps"[8] An almost similar view was expressed by Vagiswari. In her words, "Harijan children's reason for discontinuing education is in terms of their parent's poverty, ignorance of the benefits of education and lack of schools in the villages".[9]

8. C. Parvathamma, "*Paper Presented at the Parliamentary for S.C. and S.T.*, New Delhi, 1973, p. 5.

9. Vagiswari, *Income Earning Trends and Social Status of the Harijan Community in Tamil Nadu*, Sangham Publishers, Madras, 1972, pp. 11-18.

As Given by the Daughter Respondents

38.46 per cent of uneducated daughter respondents expressed the reason for their illiteracy as lack of pressure from their parents. Another reason was that they (26.92%) thought education was unnecessary for women. 23.08 per cent of them who had expressed reasons other than these said it was family responsibility. They claimed that their presence was inevitable at home to look after the children and household, and hence they could not attend schools. The remaining 11.54 per cent of the respondents reported that economic handicap was their main obstacle.

As Given by the Mother Respondents

53.15 per cent of the mother respondents gave financial problem as the main reason for discontinuing their studies. 30.77 per cent thought that education was unnecessary for women, 6.99 per cent gave lack of pressure from parents as the reason and 4.90 per cent gave the reason as family responsibility. It is interesting to note that 4 mothers (2.80%) expressed that although they wanted to study, they had to suffer illtreatment from higher caste teachers at school, 1.40 per cent gave the reason of school being far away from their houses.

It is generally accepted that children's literacy level depends upon the literacy of their parents. If the parent is literate, it is more likely that the child will be not only literate but also will have chances of getting higher levels of education. Another fact is that their socio-economic conditions were also favourable towards having more facilities for education. The uneducated mothers more probably were traditional workers and the wage they got was not sufficient for their family. So they had difficulty in paying their children's expenses for education. As a result, economic handicap made hindrance for education in the older generation.

The caste system and it's restrictions was another reason

given by the mothers. In early days education was the monopoly of higher castes and the lower castes were kept off from the sphere of education, which was the main hindrance that prevented them from coming up educationally. Further the Scheduled Castes gave more imortance to occupation than education. In childhood itself they began to practise work on fields and earn money, hence their lack of interest in schooling.

"Even though education of the Scheduled Castes has been made completely free of cost and the students are provided with scholarships, hostel facilities etc., most of the really poor families are unable to avail themselves of these, because sending children to school means lossing an earning hand, which they can ill-afford".[10]

It was also found that for age groups of 60-69 (1.89%) and 70+ had the reason as distance of school and both these groups had the problem of illtreatment from high-castes Hindu teachers. In older days there were no school in rural areas. If there were any schools, Scheduled Castes were not admitted there. High caste teachers were also not prepared to teach them. Owing to these reasons, the tendency of not attending school gets stronger as age increases. These findings support the findings of Dr. Rajagopalan's study. "Nearly one half of the respondents reported that they have difficulties in sending their children to school. The difficulties are of different sorts. Often what it means is that there is none else at home to care for the infants, or to guard the house. In other cases there is no school within walking distance and sending children by bus costs money and bothersome. Sometimas it is also difficult to feed the children at the lunch time as the parents

10. Sunanda Patwardhan, *Aspects of Social Mobility Among Scheduled Castes in Paona*, Ph.D. Thesis, Poona University, 1966, p. 90.

would have locked the house and been away at work. But mainly the difficulties are financial."[11]

The main difference between two generations was that daughter's generation did not have the problem of the school being far or suffer illtreatment from high caste teachers. It may be noted that owing to governmental efforts, new schools were built up in rural areas and Scheduled Castes had more freedom to move in public places. Today untouchability is not a common practice and nobody dares to hurt Scheduled Castes for fear of legal punishment. Another difference is that when financial problem was an important reason for the illiteracy of mothers, it was not so in the case of daughters. Today Government has implemented many educational facilities for Scheduled Castes. This will lessen the intensity of their economic handicap. As compared to elder generation, the younger generation can utilize more facilities. Another plus point in favour of the younger generation is that they had educated mothers who took interest in their education.

Educational Mobility among the Respondents

In the first place, we shall examine the educational level of the respondent's mothers. The majority of them i.e., 63.56 per cent, were illiterate, 23.56 per cent had primary education and 7.56 per cent had upper primary education. It was interesting to note that only 2.67 per cent of the mother respondents were having high school education, 1.78 per cent had completed SSLC and one per cent was having college education. The extreme educational backwardness of the earlier generation of Scheduled Caste women is revealed here.

When we turn from the respondent's mothers to the respondents themselves, a profound change could be noticed. As against 63.56 per cent mothers, the percentage of daughters without education, came down to 11.55 per cent. 88.45 per

11. C. Rajagopalan, *Social Mobility Among the Scheduled Castes*, Banglore, University I.C.S.R. Report, 1978, p. 109.

cent had moved up the educational ladder. At the same time, the increase in the number of educated respondents was indeed remarkable as compared to the educated mothers. It was also noteworthy that between mothers and daughters, there was an increase in the percentage at all levels of education except at the primary level, with the highest increase in the college level, followed by SSLC, High School and Upper Primary. Thus, there was hardly any doubt that the daughters had better education than their mothers.

We shall now examine the rate of inter-generational mobility between the respondents' mother's generation and the respondents' generation. The data relating to this is presented in Table No. 10.

The process of educational mobility could be understood from the above table. It could be seen that as many 143 out of 225 or 63.56 per cent of the respondent's mothers will be illiterate. But the 143 illiterate mothers had only 13.28 per cent respondents (daughters) were illiterate. In the remaining 86.72 per cent, the children had education higher than their mothers. While 20.98 per cent had high school education, 38.46 per cent has SSLC education and 4.20 per cent had even college education. Similarly, out of the 53 mothers with primary education, only 9.43 per cent of their children were without any education. Out of the 90.57 per cent, only 13.21 per cent of the children had the same level of education as their mothers. The remaining 77.36 per cent of children had gone up the educational ladder in variant degrees i.e. 5.66 per cent had upper primary, 49.06 per cent had high school, 13.21 per cent had SSLC and 9.43 per cent had college education. Of the 17 mothers with upper primary education, 11.76 per cent were illiterate, 87 24 per cent cases of the children had a higher educational level than their mothers. Lastly, of the 12 mothers with high school and above level of enucation, their children also had education one level higher their mothers. But there

TABLE 10

Inter-generational Educational Mobility.

Mothers' education	Daughters' Education						
	Illiterates	*Primary*	*Upper Primary*	*High School*	*SSLC*	*College*	*Total*
Illiterate	19 13.28%	6 4.20%	27 18.88%	30 20.98%	55 38.46%	6 4.20%	143 63.55%
Primary	5 9.43%	7 13.21%	3 5·66%	26 49.06%	7 13.21%	5 9.43%	53 23.56%
Upper primary	2 11.76%	—	—	4 23.53%	5 29.41%	6 35.29%	17 7.56%
High School	—	—	—	—	2 33.33%	4 66.97%	6 2.67%
SSLC	—	—	—	—	2 50.00%	2 50.00%	4 1.78%
College	—	—	—	—	—	2 100.00%	2 0.88%
Total	26 11.55%	13 5.78%	30 13.33%	60 26.67%	71 31.56%	25 11.11%	225

was not to be seen a single case where children of mothers with high school and above education were illiterates. Another finding from this table is that the proportion of respondents with higher education increased with increase in the educational level of their own mothers. Conversely, the proportion of illiterates decreased with the increase in the educational level of the mothers. The former trend is visible in the level of high school education and above. The influence of mother's education on the daughter's educational level was quite evident i.e., the level of education of the mothers was found to have a positive influence on the education of daughters. This was because the educated mothers know the value and need of education for their children in future, so that they encouraged their children's educational ambitions and aspirations. The phenomenon of highly educated mothers having illiterate daughters was totally absent. These findings support the hypothesis that there is considerable educational mobility between these two generations of Scheduled Caste women.

Awareness About Welfare Measures

There were many efforts taken by the State Government for the upliftment of Scheduled Castes in Kerala. The major efforts are educational programmes for Scheduled Castes, programmes for removing untouchability, housing etc. The educational programmes include fee concessions, scholarships, stipends, free books, payment of examination fees, grant in aid for maintenance of schools, hostels, boarding houses, orphanages, reading rooms and libraries intended for backward communities. Education consumed the lion's share of the expenditure incurred on Harijan Welfare.

When we enquired about the awareness of educational facilities provided to Scheduled Castes by the Government during their student days, it was found that majority (66.67%) of mothers were not aware of these facilities. Mother's age has some influence on the awareness of these facilities. Mother's age groups were more aware about the welfare measures than older age groups. Within the mother's group, it was found that as the age increased the level of awareness decreased.

It may be noted that the younger generation was influenced by modern education. The mass media also had a significant role in making them aware of these facilities. Now-a-days even, illiterate mothers are aware of these facilities. This may be due to modern means of communication like radio, television etc., and from other sources like local friends or neighbours giving publicity about the welfare measures specially made for Scheduled Castes.

On our enquiry about the sources of information, it was found that out of 75 mothers (who were aware of educational facilities) 69.33 per cent got information from teachers, 18.67 per cent from neighbours, 2.67 per cent from radio and 9.33 per cent had its source from newspapers. In the case of mothers only the educated had awareness of welfare measures. It was observed that the majority of the educated group among mothers got information from teachers. This may be because the intimation regarding all the welfare measures was put up in notice boards both in schools and colleges.

In the case of daughters, they got information from the same source. The change between two generations is that in the daughters generation even the illiterates were well informed about the welfare measures when compared to mothers. Cent per cent of daughter respondents of our study were aware of welfare measures. Those who were educated got information from mass media and communication. It was found that cent per cent of daughters were in the higher income group ie. Rs. 400 and above.

Mother's level of education also had influence on the awareness of welfare measures. Our study made clear that the highly educated grups were more aware of educational welfare measures. Among the illiterate mothers nobody was aware of the facilities. But as education increased, the number of persons who were aware of the welfare measures also increased. The literate respondents become aware of government's welfare measures through reading newspapers or from other mass media of communications and coorrespondence with others.

Utilization of Welfare Measures

The government of India Act 1935, which first identified Scheduled Castes and Scheduled Tribes stressed the need for special attention to the welfare and uplift of these classes. But only proper and adequate utilization of the welfare measures can bring about the desired effect. Shantha Kumari in her study on 'Scheduled Caste and Welfare Measures' made clear that "Scheduled Castes are eager to make full use of the facilities given by the Government. But because the children fail countinuously, they find it difficult to meet their expenses in the absense of lumpsum grant and exception from fees at secondary school level, and then they are forced to stop their studies. This prevents them from availing the facilities any further. One of the reasons for the inadequate utilization of educational facilities by the Scheduled Castes is the ignorance about the potential which education holds for improving their life chances".[12]

We found that among the 33.33 per cent of mothers who were aware of educational facilities, 28.05 per cent had not utilized them. But 42.68 per cent of them had made partial utiliazation and 28.27 per cent had full utilization. The educated mothers were found to be using the educational facilities more. The following Table illustrate this point.

12. Shanthakumari, "*Scheduled Caste and Welfare Measures*" Classical Publishing Company, New Delhi, pp. 86-87.

TABLE 11

Mothers' Education and Utilization of Eeducational Facilities

Mothers' Education	*Utiltzation of Educational Facilities*			
	No utilization	*Partial utilization*	*Full utilization*	*Total*
Primary	18 33.86%	25 47.17%	10 18.87%	53 64.63%
Upper Primary	5 29.41%	8 47.06%	4 22.53%	17 20.73%
High School	—	2 33.33%	4 66.67%	6 7.32%
S.S.L.C.	—	—	4 100.00%	4 4.88%
College	—	—	2 100.00%	2 2.44%
Total	23 28.05%	35 42.68%	24 29.27%	82*

*The question was applicable to only 82 Respondents who were literates.

The above table makes clear that as education increased the utilization of welfare measures also increased. This was because the educated people were more aware of the educational schemes and those who were less aware of the schemes. It could be seen that the findings of the present study were in tune with that of S.K Yadav (1983) ie., "the more educated respondents, when they passed from one class to another, automatically received these facilities".[13]

13. S.K. Yadav, *Harijan Awareness of Education Schemes*, The Academic Press, Haryana, 1983, p. 87.

The relation between age and utilization of educational facilities reveals that cent per cent of the younger generation fully availed themselves of the facilites offered.

The position regarding the elder generation is given below.

TABLE 12

Mother's Age and Utilization of Educational Facilities

Mothers' age	*Utilization of Educational Facilities*			
	No utilization	*Partial utilization*	*Full utilization*	*Total*
Below 40	—	—	6 100.00%	6 7.32%
40—49	—	25 58.14%	18 41.86%	43 42.44%
50—59	16 61.54%	10 38.46%	—	26 31.71%
60—69	3 100.00%	—	—	3 3.66%
70+	4 100.00%	—	—	4 4.87%
Total	23 28.05%	35 42.68%	24 29.27%	82*

*The question was applicable to only 82 rcspondents who were literates.

All the respondents below 40 age group availed themselves of the full use of the educational facilities. But in the case of elder generation nobody made utilization of the welfare measures. As age increased, the utilization of eduational facilities decreased. This may be because in early days welfare measures in terms of education were not implemented for the benefit of the Scheduled Castes, and hence the elder generation was not able to utilize them. But in recent period, changes in the attitude of teachers, governmental efforts for removing social evils etc. have helped a lot in utilizing these facilities. So younger generation got more chance for availing themselves of facilities then older generation.

In the three districts from which the samples were selected, the utilization pattern seemed to differ. In Alleppey we found maximum utilization of facilities (55.26%), 47.73 per cent of respondents from Trivandrum also utilized the facilities and cent per cent of respondents from Palghat were illiterate, so it was not applicable to them. This provides ample evidence to the fact that the educationally forward respondents made maximum utilization of facilities and vice versa. In the case of daughter respondents cent per cent of them fully utilized them. Today, parents are more aware of the value of edcation and they show more interest in their children's studies. Besides, Government's new and attractive welfare measures and policies help them to attend school. School and college teachers, information from school notice boards etc. help them to utilize these facilities.

Level of Educational Aspiration of the generations

Level of aspiration is a determining factor in the formation and achievement of goals, in the life of individuals.

We therefore examined the level of aspiration for education of both mothers and daughters.

The above Table makes clear that 63.11 per cent of mothers wanted only to learn how to read and write. At the same time, 88.89 per cent of their daughters desired to study up to the degree level. The vast intergenerational difference in the level of aspiration can be observed here. Older generation had low level of aspiration and younger generation were highly ambitious. The younger generation was more aware of the social value of education in the society. The parents who took

TABLE 13

Level of Educational Aspiration of Mother's and Daughiers.

Level of educational aspirations	*Mothers'*	*Daughters'*	*Total*
For reading and writing	142 63.71%	16 7.11%	158 35.11%
S.S.L.C.	68 30.22%	9 4.00%	77 17.11%
P.D.C.	3 1.33%	—	3 0.67%
Degree	12 5.33%	200 88.89%	212 47.11%
Total	225 100.00%	225 100.00%	450

an interest in the education of their childeren also motivated the younger generation for high aspirations. "The importance of education as a means of achieving upward social mobility is grasped by the Harijans and there is a conscious effort on their part to get their children educated"[14]

Motivation for Higher Education

In rural areas parents are mostly illiterate, economically poor, socially depressed, busy day and night in earning their bread and also educational facilities like schools are not available in a number of places. So, parents have practically no time for thinking about education. As a consequence, the students of rural areas do not take interest in education.

It was interesting to examine who motivated our respondents for higher education. This question was raised only to

14. Sunanda Patwardhan, *Change Among India's Harijans*, Orient Longman Ltd., 1973, New Delhi, p. 80.

those who had above S.S.L.C. education. In the case of mother respondents only two of them were college educated. Of these two, one was self motivated and the other by parents.

Among the daughter respondents, 25 out of the total respondents were college educated. Out of this, 36 per cent were motivated by parents. It had been proved that the educated parents were in a better position to provide their children with the right guidance and advice and thus motivate them for higher education. The remaining 28 per cent were motivated by teachers, another 20 per cent of them by others like nuns, landlords (whose servants they had been), 12 per cent by friends, and 4 per cent was self motivated.

Usually in the lower levels, it is the parents who take initiative in their children's education. In the case of the 36 per cent who were motivated by the parents, the parents had modern education.

Objectives and Aims in Education

Ottaway defines "education as an activity which goes on in a society and its aim and methods depends on the nature of society in which it takes place".[15] The aim of education is synonymous with aim of human life.

TABLE 14

Mothers' and Daughters' Aim of Education

Aim of education	*Mothers'*	*Daughters'*	*Total*
To get a job	5 41.67%	110 70.51%	115 68.45%
To improve status	7 58.33%	46 29.49%	53 31.55%
Total	12 100.00%	156 100.00%	168

15. A.K.C. Ottaway, *Education and Society*, Routledge and Kegan Paul Ltd., New York, 1960, p. 1.

The aims of education given by the respondents are to get a job and to improve status. The following Table gives the data regarding the objectives of education given by the mothers and daughters.

With regard to the objectives of education of Scheduled Caste women, the question was raised only to those who had high school and above level of education. In the case of mothers, majority (58.33%) gave the aim of education as to improve status. But their daughter's aim of education was to get a job. Here we can see the deviation within two generations regarding the aim of education. The elder generation wanted to improve their status through education, because they were denied of education in older days and they thought that education can improve their social status. But the younger generation gave importance to modern occupation. They thought education was helpful for attaining government jobs. They wanted any non traditional job and a high income through education. This shows that they knew that education was an important factor for white collar jobs.

The educational level of the respondents and their perceived aim of education were found to be related to each other. The Table No. 15 makes it clear.

The Table made clear that the daughters gave importance to getting a job as the aim of education. The younger generation viewd education as a direct means to employment and economic betterment. The higher the education of the daughters, the higher was their brief that education was a means for getting modern job. The X^2 test showed significant relation between these two, well beyond at .01 level. We further applied contingency coefficient, the result of which established the dependency between these two characteristics.

TABLE 15

Daughters' Level of Education and Their Aim in Education

Daughters' education	*Aim of Education*		
	To get a job	*To improve status*	*Total*
High School	33 55.00%	27 45.00%	60 38.46%
S.S.L.C	54 76.06%	17 23.94%	71 45.51%
College	23 92.00%	2 8.00%	25 16.03%
Total	100 70.51%	46 29.49%	156

$X^2 = 15.82$

Degree of Freedom=2

Table value at .01 level=9.210

C=0.303

In the case of mothers also, education seemed to influence the aim of education.

TABLE 16

Mothers' Level of Education and Aim in Education

Education of mother respondents	*Aim in Education*		
	To get a job	*To improve status*	*Total*
High School	4 66.67%	2 33.33%	6 30.00%
S.S.L.C	1 25.00%	3 75.00%	4 33.33%
College	—	2 100.00%	2 16.67%
Total	5 41.67%	7 58.33%	12*

*Only 12 mothers were having high school and above level of education.

The majority of the respondents viewed that education had only one objective viz., to improve status. They believed that the miseries and sufferings their fore-fathers had to endure had been due to illiteracy and it made them to consider education as a means of improving their own status and that of their caste. 41.67 per cent of the mother respondents considered that it was education that helped them in getting jobs which might be indirectly associated with the improvement of economic status.

Advantage of Education

When asked about their opinion about the advantages of education, they expressed three advantages viz., education helps to get a job, helps to improve status, helps to get a good alliance in marriage.

The opinion in this regard was seen to be influenced by age and education. As age increased, the desire to achieve status improvement also increased. Both X^2 value and contingency coefficient showed significant relationship. The following Table will make it clear.

From the above table it was found that the majority of the younger generation of below 20 age group, (70.18%) said that the most important advantage of education was that it helped them to get a modern job. At the same time, majority of the elder generation of above 50 age group, (64.70%) expressed the advantage of education as a status raising factor. It can he noted that the younger age group was having a clear idea about the advantage of education for getting non-traditional jobs. But the elder age group felt that the factor which was responsible for their backwardness was lack of education, so they thought that education could raise their status in society.

The opinion of mothers also was analysed on the basis of age. The following Table will make the result.

TABLE 17

Daughter's Age and Advantages of Education

Daughter's age	*Advantages of Education*			
	Helps to get a job	*Helps to improve status*	*Helps to get a good marriage alliance*	*Total*
Below 20	40 70.18%	10 17.54%	7 12.28%	57 25.33%
20—29	47 61.84%	20 26.32%	9 11.84%	76 33.78%
30—39	22 48.89%	17 37.78%	6 13.33%	45 20.00%
40—49	13 43.33%	15 50.00%	2 6.67%	30 13.33%
50+	3 17.65%	11 64.70%	3 17.65%	17 7.55%
Total	125 55.56%	73 32.44%	27 12.30%	225

$X^2=41.68$

DF=8

Table value at ,01 level=20.090

C=0.395

TABLE 18

Mothers' Age and Advantage of Education

Mothers' age	*Advantages of Education*			
	Helps to get a job	*Helps to improve status*	*Helps to get good alliance in marriage*	*Total*
Below 40	3 15.00%	15 80.00%	1 5.00%	20 8.89%
40—49	3 4.55%	59 89.39%	4 6.06%	66 29.33%
50—59	3 4.84%	57 91.93%	1 3.23%	62 27.55%
60—69	1 1.79%	55 98.21%	—	56 24.89%
70+	—	21 100.00%	—	21 9.33%
Total	10 4.44%	208 92.44%	7 3.11%	225

It is seen from this Table that the majority in the mothers' generation in all age groups considered education as a means of status improvement. In the case of youngsters, they considered education as having some other advantages like a means for getting good marriage alliance etc. The older generation did not get education because of the barriers in casteism, so they thought that if they were educated, they would get status through it.

From Table 19 it is clear that the better educated responpondents considered the advantage of education as a means to get modern jobs than the less educated. This Table also gives ample edvidence to the fact that educated people could envisage many other advantages of education than mearely getting a job. 20 per cent of college educated group believed that they could attain a better status through education.

TABLE 19

Daughters' Education and Advantage of Education

Daughters' education	*Advantage of education*			
	Helps to get a job	*Helps to improve status*	*Helps to get good marriage alliance*	*Total*
Illiterate	8 33.77%	15 57.69%	3 11.54%	26 11.55%
Primary	5 38.46%	6 46.15%	2 15.39%	13 5.78%
Upper Primary	12 40.00%	16 53.33%	2 6.67%	30 13.33%
High School	35 58.33%	14 23.33%	11 18.33%	60 26.67%
S.S.L.C.	45 63.38%	17 23.94%	9 12.68%	71 31.56%
College	20 80.00%	5 20.00%	–	25 11.11%
Total	125 55.56%	73 32.44%	27 12.00%	225

The same was found to be true in the case of the mothers also. The highly educated mothers thought of the advantages of education other than getting a job. The following table will make this clear.

TABLE 20

Mothers' Education and Advantages of Education

Mothers' education	*Advantage of education*			
	Helps to get a job	*Helps to improve status*	*Helps to get good marriage alliance*	*Total*
Illiterate	—	143 100.00%	—	143 63.56%
Primary	—	53 100.00%	—	53 23.56%
Upper Primary	3 17.66%	12 70.58%	2 11.76%	17 7.56%
High School	3 50.00%	—	3 50.00%	6 2.67%
S.S.L.C.	2 50.00%	—	2 50.00%	4 1.77%
College	2 100.00%	—	—	2 0.88%
Total	10 4.44%	208 92.44%	7 3.11%	225

It was found that for 50 per cent of the high school educated and SSLC educated members and cent per cent of the college educated mothers, the advantage of education was that it helped them to get a job. None of them among the highly educated considered improvement of status being an advantage of education. This might be due to the fact that educated people realised the instrumental value of education and hence could manage a modern job than the uneducated.

The data was analysed on the basis of income and was found to be related to the advantage of education. The following Table will make it clear.

TABLE 21

Daughters' Income and Advantages of Education

Income (Rs.)	*Advantages of education*			
	Helps to get a job	*Helps to improve status*	*Helps to get a good marriage alliance*	*Total*
Below 100	19 67.85%	2 27.44%	7 25.00%	28 12.44%
101—200	73 68.23%	25 23.36%	9 8.41%	107 47.55%
201—300	17 41.47%	22 53.66%	2 4.87%	41 18.22%
301—400	6 37.50%	8 50.00%	2 12.50%	16 7.11%
401—500	2 25.00%	4 50.00%	2 25.00%	8 3.56%
501—600	2 33.33%	3 50.00%	1 16.67%	6 2.61%
601—700	4 44.44%	3 33.33%	2 22.22%	9 4.00%
700+	2 20.00%	6 60.00%	2 20.00%	10 4.44%
Total	125 55.56%	73 32.44%	27 12.00%	225

X^2=39.095

D.F.=14

Table value at .01 level=29.141

C=0.39

From the above Table it is seen that the lower income group considered education as a means for earning money, getting jobs. In the higher income group i.e. (above Rs. 700) 60 per cent expressed the advantage as to improve status. At the same time, only 7.14 per cent of below Rs. 100 income group had the same opinion.

The higher income group thought that occupational advancement gave them equal status in society. Since they had money, the immediate question before them was about discarding the traditional inferior caste status. For the lower income group, to earn a living was an absolute need and hence they could only think of education as a means of giving them a modern job with reasonable remuneration.

In the case of mothers also the trend was not different. Majority of (98.46%) the lowest income group i.e. below Rs. 100 per month were of the opinion that the most important advantage of education was that it helped to get a job, whereas in the case of the highest income group i.e., above Rs. 700, cent per cent of them gave importance to education as a status raising factor.

Level of Education of the Children of Both Generations

27.42 per cent of the children of the daughter respondents were studying at primary level, 24.19 per cent were at upper primary level and 45.16 per cent were at high school level and 3.23 per cent were at S.S.L.C. level. And all of them were availing educational facilities provided by Government. None of them was staying away from house for educational purpose.

23.73 per cent of the children of mother respondents were studying at High School level, 38.98 per cent were at SSLC level and 6.78 per cent were PDC level and 28.8 per cent were at Degree level and the remaining 1.69 per cent were doing professional courses. These mothers were of the younger age group and highly educated. In this group also nobody was staying outside for educational purpose and all of them were getting educational facilities from the Government.

The above facts prove that the younger generation of the Scheduled Castes was continuing their education all were availing themselves of Government welfare programmes for them.

Educational Aspirations for Their Sons and Daughters

All the mother respondents, when asked to what educational levels their children should rise, expressed the desire that their male children would be educated to any extend the desired. Even older people who at one stage were not aware of the importance of education or had no interest, were very much interested in the education of their children. Khan's study also observed a similar change in the thinking of the adult Harijans of Santur village in Bangalore district.[16] 57.78 per cent of mother respondents agreed that their daughters should study up to the extent they desire. 42.22 per cent did not favour education for girls, and they belonged to the older age group and had the reason that girls would not benefit much from education. They had the traditional views of assigning the role of home management to the girls. Majumdar (1950) has made a similar observation that "the villagers think that girls do not need education, the argument being that sooner or later they will marry and settle down in their homes and any knowledge they receive of history or geography."[17]

As against the view of the mothers, the daughter respondents expressed the wish to educate both their sons and daughters to the maximum extent possible. They accounted illiteracy to be the reason for their backwardness, both social

16. Mumtaz Ali Khan, "Impact of the Constitutional Protection and Safeguards on the Scheduled Castes at Santur Village", *Economic Review*, May 15, Vol. 20, 1969, pp. 13-17.

17. D.N. Majumdar, *Report on the Sociological Stalus of Castes and Tribes of Gujarat*, 1950, p. 12.

and economic. They were convinced that education enabled the boys and girls for better prospects in life. So they wanted their children to gain knowledge through education. Malik observes that "the Scheduled Castes believe that by giving their children education, they will move away from the low traditional caste-based occupations, and thereby achieve a higher status. She continues that respondents have realised the importance of education because it enables them to achieve a higher status and leads to the abandonment of caste based occupations.".[18]

Education and Social Status

"Status is the position that a person occupies on the scale or ladder of esteem in the eyes of other members of his society. Status depended on a variety of factors such as birth, wealth, ability, occupation, type of education etc. Everybody's status is the outcome of how other people assess his roles and the way he plays them."[19] Statistical indicators such as literacy, education and employment, political participation, age at marriage and other demographic features help to determine the status of women.

A rise in literacy and educational attainment of a class of people is a reliable indicator of change in their status. In the case of Scheduled Caste women, the formidable barrier in the way of assessing change is that they have been under constant influences of traditional values and patterns of behaviour of higher castes and education was never considered a must for women who were not expected to play modern roles in the society.

To find out whether the respondents thought of education as a status raising factor, we asked some specific questions. When

18. Suneila Malik, *Social Integration of Scheduled Castes*, Abhinav Publications, New Delhi, 1979, pp. 56-101.
19. Mary Douglass, *Man in Society*, Adults Book Ltd., London, 1964, p. 80.

enquired about their views on women's education there was a vast difference between the views of the mothers and daughters.

TABLE 22

Mothers' and Daughters' Views on Women's Education.

Views on education	*Mother's*	*Daughter's*	*Total*
Must	56	156	212
	24.89%	69.33%	47.11%
Necessary	105	67	172
	46.67%	29.78%	38.22%
Unnecessary	64	2	66
	28.44%	0.89%	14.67%
Total	225	225	450
	100.00%	100.00%	

When majority of the (47%) mothers thought that education was necessary, 69 per cent of daughters said that it was a 'must'. It is interesting to note that 28.44 per cent mothers thought that women's education was unnecessary. The younger generation had a more favourable attitude towards education than the elder generation. This may be due to the fact that the younger generation was educated and was economically better. They were aware of the educational facilities, as also the reservation for Harijans in Government and public undertakings.

Another point we found was that, 35.56 per cent of the mothers and 78.11 per cent of the daughters considered education as a 'must' for securing good job. The following Table shows the opinion of mother's and daughter's regarding this aspect.

There was remarkable difference in the opinion of these two generations. While only 35.56 per cent of the mothers thought

TABLE 23

Mothers' and Daughters' Opinion About Education and Job

Opinion about education and job	*Mothers*	*Daughter*	*Total*
Least importont	13 5.78%	—	13 2.89%
Less important	46 20.44%	7 3.11%	53 11.78%
Important	86 38.22%	40 17.78%	126 28.00%
Highly important	80 35.56%	178 79.11%	258 57.33%
Total	225 100.00%	225 100.00%	450

that education was highly important for a good job, 79.11 per cent of daughters said it was so. From this, it is clear that the younger generation was more aware of the necessity of education for securing a good job than the elder generation. They also thought that when educational status increased, their occupational status also increased and through this they might get social acceptance in society.

Our analysis showed that age, education and the response were related to each other i.e. none among the daughters thought that education was not a must for securing a good job. Majority (96.49%) of below 20 age group considered that education was a must for securing a good job, when only 23.53 per cent of above 50 age group said so. This may be because the younger age group was aware of the role of education in securing a modern job with reasonable remuneration and they were aware of the competition existing in this field.

Mothers of younger age group i.e. below 40 (50%) thought that education was highly important for securing a good job. In the case of elder age group (70+ age group) only 9.52 per cent thought so. The majority of these groups considered that education was of least importance for securing a good job. This also showed that younger age group realised the important role and value of education.

It was also found that as the level of education increased, those who thought about education being a must for a good job, also increased. Among the illiterate daughters 53.85 per cent considered education being highly important for securing a good job. It is also seen that cent per cent of SSLC and college educated groups considered education as a must for a good job. It is interesting to note that in the second generation respondents even when they were illiterates, considered that education was not must for securing job. Thus we can infer that the level of education of the respondents and their opinion regarding the role of education in getting good job were much related.

The response of the mothers was not different from this i.e. among the illiterates, 9.09 per cent considered that education was of least importance for securing a good job, and 24.48 per cent of the same group that it was less important. Cent per cent of higher educated groups such as the high school, the SSLC and the college educated considered education as a must for securing a good job. They thought that education led to the abandonment of caste-based occupations and unfolded before them various occupational advancement. The educated women were more aware of the need for education for securing jobs.

Education as a Status Raising Facto

From the analysis of our data it could be observed that majority of the respondents, both mothers and daughters, of all educational categories regarded education as an important criterion for status improvement. They were making the utmost efforts to bestow education to their children so as to raise their social status. For comparing mothers' and daughters' responses the data was analysed and it was found that 40.89 per cent of mother respondents and 89.33 per cent of daughter respondents considered education being important for status improvement.

It was found that cent per cent of the younger age group of daughters considered education as a must in raising social status. In the case of the elder age group above 50 (29.42%) opined that education was of least importance for social status. It is interesting to note that in the same age group 29.42 per cent expressed that education was highly important for securing status in society. This might be because, that group might have higher education through which, they attained status in society.

In the case of mothers, the data was analysed on the basis of age, education, income and caste. Caste and income of the respondents did not seem to influence their attitude in this case. A large majority (85.32%) of mothers considered education as an important factor for status improvement. A majority (60%) of younger generations (below 40 age group) regarded education as an important criterion for social status. From this it may be noted that younger generation felt that with education they could attain status through modern occupation.

The education wise analysis of daughters' data showed that a majority of all educational categories regarded education as an important criterion for improving status except illiterates. Among the illiterates 30.76 per cent of them also considered it in the sgme way. It is clear that the highly educated group felt that with education they and their children could be able to get modern occupation, so as to raise social status.

Both the mother's and daughter's data were analysed on

the basis of income and they followed a similar trend. In both the generations, the higher income group fully believed that education was highly important for raising status. This was because in both the generations, the higher income groups were having non traditional occupations that fetched them higher status hence they considered education as a status raising factor.

When asked whether they thought education could improve their living condition, cent per cent of the daughters agreed with it. This may be because, as a result of education, they thought they would get jobs which would lead to their economic independence. In the case of mothers, 71.11 per cent said that education could improve living condition. In this group the respondent's age and education were found influencing them. The younger age and the highly educated groups were having positive attitude. 80 per cent of the below 40 age group that they could improve their living condition through education. At the same time, only 67.86 per cent in the 60—69 age group and 66 67 per cent of the 70+age group thought so. This may be because they were aware of the fact that education was a status raising factor, Educated persons had more chances for modern occupation which would naturally raise their living condition.

Education and Acceptance from Members of Other Castes

To a question 'Do you feel that education helps to get more acceptance from members of other castes ?, 45.77 per cent of the mothers and 60 per cent of the daughters gave a positive answer. The Table no. 23 analyses the difference of opinion that education helps to get more acceptance from other castes.

The difference of opinion regarding the above issue showed the influence of education on Scheduled Castes. The younger generation was educated and they got more social acceptance from society than the elder generation. Today in public places, offices, and schools, there is no discrimination on the basis of

TABLE 23

Mothers' and Daughters' Opinion on Education and Acceptance from Other Castes.

Whether education contributes to acceptance from other castes	*Mothers'*	*Daughters'*	*Total*
Yes	103 45.78%	135 60.00%	238 52.89%
No	122 54.22%	90 40.00%	212 47.11%
Total	225 100.00%	225 100.00%	450

caste and among them, the educated get more chance for enjoying such freedom. That was why the second generation opined that education helped to get more acceptance from members of other castes.

Both the responses were analysed on the basis of age, education, income and occupation. As age increased, the number of daughter respondents who said that education helped to get more acceptance from members of other castes, decreased. In the younger age group (below 20 yers) 66.67 per cent said that they felt education helped to get more acceptance from members of other castes, while in the 50+ age group only 41.18 per cent opined similarly. The latter age group were illiterates and were unaware of the value of education, so they expressed the above opinion.

The Table no. 24 makes it clear that 90 per cent of the below 40 age group mothers agreed that they would get acceptance from the members of other castes by education. At the same time, in the above 70 age group, only 28.57 per cent agreed with that. A majority (71.43%) in this group did not

TABLE 24

Mothers' Age and Opinion on Education and Acceptance from Other Castes.

Mothers' Age	*Whether education contributes to acceptance from other castes*		
	Yes	*No*	*Total*
Below 40	18 90.00%	2 10.00%	20 8.89%
40—49	32 48.48%	34 51.52%	66 29.33%
50—59	29 46.77%	33 53.23%	62 27.55%
60—69	18 32.14%	38 67.86%	56 24.89%
70+	6 28.57%	15 71.43%	21 9.33%
Total	103 45.77%	122 54.22%	225

$X^2=22.66$

Degrees of freedom=4

Table value of .01 level=13.277

C=0.30

consider that education helped to get more acceptance from members of other castes. The relationship between age and their response was quite significant well beyond .01 level. A coefficient of correlation was also applied which confirmed the relationship.

The daughter's data was analysed on the basis of education and was found that as education increased, the number of respondents who said that education helped to get more acceptance from other castes, also increased. As the level of education went up, (i.e. SSLC 75 per cent, college education cent per cent) opinion that education help to get more acceptance from the members of other castes also increased. In both the generations, a similar trend could be seen and every respondent received the advantage of education as status improvement.

TABLE 25

Mothers' Education and Opinion on Education and Acceptance from Other Castes.

Mothers' education	*Whether education contributes to acceptance from other castes*		
	Yes	*No*	*Total*
Illiterate	60 41.96%	83 58.04%	143 63.56%
Primary	25 47.17%	28 52.83%	53 23.55%
Upper Primary	9 52.94%	8 47.06%	17 7.56%
High School	4 66.67%	2 33.33%	6 2.67%
S.S.L.C.	3 75.00%	1 25.00%	4 1.77%
College	2 100.00%	—	2 0.88%
Total	103 47.77%	122 54.23%	225

It is clear from the above Table that majority of illiterate members were not considering education leading to more acceptance from the members of other castes. 41.96 per cent considered education as a medium for social acceptance. In the case of the highly educated also cent per cent thought so. it is true that an educated person enjoys a greater acceptance by other castes than an uneducated person. Naturally, the educated believe that education is a good medium for social acceptance by other castes.

TABLE 26

Daughter' Occupation and Opinion on Education and Acceptance from Other Castes

Daughters' occupation	*Whether education contributes to acceptance from other castes*		
	Yes	*No*	*Total*
Professional	2 100.00%	—	2 0.88%
White collars	18 85.71%	3 14.29%	21 9.33%
Agriculture	22 56.41%	17 43.59%	39 17.33%
Other labourers	5 35.71%	9 64.29%	14 6.22%
Traditional	36 48.65%	38 51.35%	74 32.89%
Unemployed	52 69.33%	23 30.67%	75 63.33%
Total	135 60.00%	90 40.00%	225

The above Table illustrates the association between occupation and the response that education helps to get more acceptance from the members of higher castes. Cent percent of the professional workers and 85.71 per cent of the white collars agreed that education helped them to get more acceptance from other castes. In the case of traditional workers only 48.65 per cent thought so. It seemed that the white collars and the professionals had higher status in society and were getting acceptance from other castes.

TABLE 27

Mothers' Occupation and Opinion on Education and Acceptance from Other Castes.

Mothers' occupation	*Whether education contributes to acceptance from other castes*		
	Yes	*No*	*Total*
White collar	1 100.00%	—	1 0.44%
Professional	1 100.00%	—	1 0.44%
Traditional	60 39.47%	92 60.53%	152 67.56%
Agricultural	37 63.79%	21 36.21%	58 25.78%
Other labourers	1 20.00%	4 80.00%	5 2.22%
Unemployed	3 37.50%	5 62.50%	8 3.56%
Total	103 45.78%	122 54.22%	225

The Table shows that cent per cent of those belonging to the modern occupational category agreed that occupation helped to get more acceptance from members of other castes. At the same time, a majority (60.53%) of traditional workers were not thinking in those terms. It is however assumed that the white collars and the professionals had certain level of education and they were aware of the utility and the value of education. In the case of the traditional workers, they had no education, as a result of which they were unaware of the advantages of education.

Education and Acceptance from Scheduled Castes Community

When asked about the attitude of the people belonging to one's own caste towards the educated in their community, it was found that majority of (65.33%) educated mothers and 43.56 per cent of educated daughters opined that they were given more respect. The remaining 27.11 per cent of educated mothers and 31.11 per cent of educated daughters said the others were jealous of them. 25.33 per cent educated daughters and 7.56 per cent of educated mothers said that there was no

TABLE 28

Daughters' Age and Opinion of the Behaviour of Scheduled Caste People Towards the Educated

Daughters' age	*Opinion of the behaviour of Scheduled Caste people towards the educated*			
	Shows more respect	*Behaves as equals*	*Feels jealousy*	*Total*
Below 20	20 35.09%	13 22.81%	24 42.10%	57 25.33%
20—29	30 39.47%	18 23.68%	28 36.84%	76 33.78%
30—39	22 48.89%	13 28.89%	10 22.22%	45 20.00%
40—49	16 53.33%	8 26.67%	6 20.00%	30 13.33%
50+	10 50.82%	5 29.41%	2 11.77%	17 7.56%
Total	98 43.56%	57 25.33%	70 31.11%	225

difference in terms of education. We felt that an element of jealousy not only in the attitude of the uneducated section towards the educated, but also among the families of the educated.

Regarding the behaviour of the Scheduled Castes people towards the educated, within the community, it was found that in the below 20 age group 35.09 per cent said that the Scheduled Caste people showed more respect towards the educated within their community, and 42.11 per cent were of the opinion that illiterate Scheduled Caste people were jealous of the educated.

The mother's data was also analysed on the basis of age and a similar trend was seen. 45 per cent of mothers in the younger age group (below 40 age group) and 85.71 per cent in the case of the 70+ age group said that Scheduled Caste people showed more respect towards the educated in their own community,

In the younger generation, all of them were availing themselves of the educational facilities and hence there is no question of receiving respect from others. But in the older generation this was not common. With the help of educated persons, the uneducated had to fulfil certain needs. Naturally, the older generation showed respect towards the educated.

Table no. 29 shows that majority (76.92%) of illiterates believed that their people had respect for the educated within their community. It was also found that only 20 per cent of the college educated also had the same opinion. The remaining highly educated (40%) said that their people behaved towards them as equals. It seems that they always had contact with the same status group that led them to behave as equals. Educations fetched them equal status.

The mothers' data was analysed on the basis of education

TABLE 29

Daughters' Education and Opinion of the Behaviour of Scheduled Caste People Towards the Educated

Daughters' education	*Opinion of the behaviour of Scheduled Caste people towards the educated*			
	Shows more respect	*Behaves as equals*	*Feels jealousy*	*Total*
Illiterate	20 76.92%	4 15.38%	2 7.69%	26 11.55%
Primary	9 69.23%	2 15.38%	2 15.38%	13 5.78%
Upper Primary	16 53.33%	8 26.67%	6 20.00%	30 13.33%
High School	22 36.67%	18 30.00%	20 33.00%	60 26.67%
S.S.L.C.	26 36.62%	15 21.13%	30 42.25%	71 31.56%
College	5 20.00%	10 40.00%	10 40.00%	25 11.11%
Total	98 43.56%	57 25.33%	70 31.11%	225

$X^2=28.99$
Degrees of freedom=10
Table of value at .01 level=23.209
C=0.34

and it was found that a majority (68.53%) of illiterates said that the people in their community showed high respect towards the educated. In the case of the highly educated group cent per cent behaved as equals towards the educated. None of the respondents belonging to the illiterate and the primary educated group did say that they behaved as equals. It may be noted that between the illiterate group and literate group there was a wider gap. The educated people held a higher position than the illiterates. This gap forced the illiterate people to show respect to the educated.

In the case of daughters their occupation was also found to be influencing their opinion. It was found that majority of (76.19%) white collars behaved as equal, only 9.52 per cent said that the Scheduled Caste people showed respect towards the educated within their community. At the same time majority of (79.73%) traditional workers said that they showed more respect towards the educated. It seems that white collars worked with the same educational status groups, and it was quite natural that they behaved as equals. A second factor could be due to lack of education which made the traditional workers respect the educated persons within their community.

The mothers' data was also analysed in terms of their occupation and found that they were not related.

Conclusion

This chapter proves the first hypothesis that there is considerable educational mobility between the two generations of Scheduled Caste women. There is definite improvement in the educational level of Scheduled Castes. It is clear from our study that a disproportionately large number of daughter respondents were literate. 64 per cent of the members were illiterates, whereas only 12 per cent of their daughters were illiterate. That is 88 per cent of daughters were deviated and had a level of education higher than their mothers.

The major factors responsible for educational mobility were parental pressure, self-motivation, higher level of aspiration of the respondents, awareness of the advantages of education, and governmental welfare measures.

Education of the mother respondents seemed to be significantly related to the educational level of the daughter respondents i e. the higher the mother's education, the higher was the educational level of their daughters, and it is known fact that the educated parents were in a better position to provide their children with right guidance and advice and they motivate them for higher education. Among the mother respondents only one per cent were college educated and were self motivated. In the case of the daughters, 4 per cent were self motivated. Majority of daughters were motivated by parents and remaining were motivated by teachers.

The majority of mother respondents were not aware of the educational facilities at the time of their studying. In case of daughters, cent per cent of them were aware about the facilities and they fully utilized them. The reason for the full utilization of educational facilities by them was that they received the information from their teachers as well as from the school and and college notice board.

While assessing the aspirational level of the respondents in the two generations in terms of education, it was found that the younger generation was highly ambitious than the elder generation. 63 per cent of the mothers' aspirational level was limited to as acquisition of knowledge of 'how to read and write'. At the same time, 89 per cent of their daughters desired to study up to graduation. The younger generation was more conscious about the social value of education.

Regarding the views on women's education, 69 per cent of daughter respondents considered it a must, while only 25 per cent of the mothers thought so. This vast difference in opinion made clear that the educated people were aware of the value of education. 58 per cent of mothers considered education as a status improving symbol. 71 per cent of daughters' aim of education was to get a job. Here we can see the deviation within two generations. The elder generation wanted to improve their status through education, but the younger generation gave importance to modern occupation. They thought education was helpful for attaining modern jobs. It was revealed that the higher the education of the respondents, the higher was their belief that education was a means for getting modern jobs.

Another finding was that majority of younger generation said that the most important advantage of education was that it helped them to get a modern job. But in the mother's generation, the majority considered education as a means for status improvement. Youngsters expressed some other advantages of education like a means for getting good marriage alliances.

It was further found that only 36 per cent of mothers opined that education was a must for securing a good job. In the case of daughters 97 per cent gave a high importance to education for attaining job. Here also, there was a remarkable difference in the opinion of these two generations.

As far as the educational aspirations for their sons and daughters were concerned, the mother respondents wanted only their sons to go up the maximum extent possible in studies. As against the view of the mothers, the daughter respondents expressed their wish to educate both boys and girls to the maximum extent possible.

The difference in the opinion of the two generations was clear in another issue also. When only 71 per cent of mothers said that education could improve their living conditions, cent per cent of their daughters agreed with that. 46 per cent of mothers and 60 per cent of daughters had the same opinion that education helped them to get acceptance from other castes. The younger generation was more educated and they got more social acceptance from society than the elder generation.

But with regard to their own community's reaction to its educated members it was found that majority of (65%) mothers and 44 per cent of daughters said they showed much respect. The disparity between the educated and the uneducated within the younger generation was less.

The above findings indicate that there was considerable change in the educational level and in the attitude of the two generations of Scheduled Caste women.

CHAPTER IV

Occupational Mobility

Caste and Occupation

Birth is the decisive criterion of membership in a caste. The origin of caste system in the Varnashrama Dharma. Historically untouchables were abhojyana (not allowed interdining) and stood out of the varna system. They lived outside the high-caste localities and were known as avarnas. The concept of pollution was attempted on them and they were treated as untouchables. These castes were systematically listed in the 1931 Census of India, and officially defined as Depressed Castes in 1932. The entire social system was governed by Brahminical law which was regressive and the avarnas were in subjection and perpetual poverty.

In the traditional Indian social system, occupation were allotted on the basis of caste. The occupations depended on the hierarchical order of caste. Each caste had its own status.

The categorization of occupation depended on caste status. The higher caste people were enjoying higher levels of occupation. Within the caste, there was also gradation, i.e. sub-division within the caste, and each in term had their own traditional occupation. There was also division of labour among sub-castes. But occupations within the main castes were homogenous and interchangeable.

The relationship between caste and occupation was particularly close in the case of Scheduled Castes. The most unclean and the least remunerative of occupations such as scavengers, leather workers, coolies were assigned to them.

Occupational Mobility

For the purpose of enquiry, we have taken occupational mobility as a shift in the occupation of the two generations of Scheduled Caste women. Occupational mobility acts not only as an indicator of social change but also as a transmitting agent of new attitudes and behaviour.

Inter generational mobility occurs betwen generations. A study of inter generational mobility focusses on the extent to which children did not inherit the occupational levels of their parents.

An occupational classification of Scheduled Castes would be necessary to know the changes in Scheduled Caste's occupational pattern. In the present study we had nine Scheduled Castes viz., Pulaya, Kurava, Mannan or Vannans, Vedar, Sambava, Thandan, Cheramar, Kanakkna, Cheruman or Cherumakkal. Traditionally, the Pulayas, Kuravas, Vedars, Cherumars, Kanakkans, Cherumans or Cherumakkals were engaged in agriculture. Kuravas were engaged in totooing also. According to Edgar Thurston, "The Mannan women were working as midwives like those of Velakkathalawan and Velar castes"[1] Vannan's or Mannan's traditional occupation is washing clothes, Thandans and Mannans are not agricultural communities. Thandan's traditional occupation is palm tree climbing while their women work on fields. Thandan women are also skilled in palm leaf climbing which gave them additional work and income. Paraiyans or, as they are commonly termed Pariahs, are traditionally drum-beaters and their women are engaged in cane work, mat weaving etc. They also go for occupation i.e., agriculture. It can be assumed that there is scope for occupational change only in a society where new occupations emerge. The occupational changes are due to the impact of industrialisation, formal education and specialised nature of skills on occupation etc. It can be regarded as measure of social change, if the Scheduled Castes have been able to gain a change of occupations.

In this study, the classification of occupation has been made under five categories :

(i) white collar,,

(ii) Professional

(iii) Traditional

(iv) Agricultural labour, and

(v) other labour.

A word of explanation about each one of these categories will be very relevant. In our study, white collar include clerks, technical workers, typists etc. Professional occupation includes teachers, doctors, nurses, and engineers etc.

Traditional occupations refer to the polluted or defiling occupations such as that of scavangers, cobblers, skinning, carcas removal, drum beating, etc., with which the Scheduled Castes have been traditionally associated. These occupations are ranked the lowest in status. Agricultural labourers are

1. Edgar Thurston, *Castes and Tribes of Southern India,* Vol. IV, Cosmo Publications, New Delhi, 1975, p. 318.

persons who are engaged in operations connected with cultivation either in paddy fields or gardens. Their work includes ploughing, tilling, transplantation, weeding, harvesting, manuring, carrying manures and any other work connected with agriculture.

Other labourers include persons working on daily wages in work other than agriculture i.e., coolie, loading labourers, construction workers, fish sellers etc.

Present Occupation of the Respondents

"Occupation may be defined as the relatively continuous patterns of activities that provide an individual or livelihood and define his/her general social status."[2]

Considering that the bulk of the population of the Scheduled Castes were illiterates, engaged in lowly occupations which yield extremely low incomes, it was necessary for their women folk to seek work. It has been shown by D'Souza that "the employment of women is the highest in the category of heads house-holds in the occupations of lowest prestige, because their women would be compelled to enter the working force for the sake of earning a living. These women workers are engaged in jobs involving very little skill and of the lowest prestige consistent with the status or occupations of their husbands. He has further tried to show that when the socio-economic condition of the husband improves, the education and training of women to fit them for jobs consistent with their status have been greatly neglected. There is usually a wide gulf between the educational qualifications of husbands and wives. Consequently, where the husband is holding a job of higher prestige by virtue of his training and qualifications, his less educated wife has fewer chances of securing a job consistent with the family status than the wife of an unskilled labourer. This

2. Y.B. Abbasayulu, *Scheduled Cast Elite*, Book Links Corporation, Hyderabad, 1978, p. 79-80.

appears to be the main reason why the rate of employment of women is highest in the category of heads of households in the occupations of lowest prestige"[3] These findings, in general, were found to be true in case of present study.

In our study, 3.56 per cent of the mother respondents and one third of (33.33%) of the daughter respondents were not going outside for work. In the case of unemployed mothers their husbands were in government service and were having high income. So there is no need for them to go out for menial jobs. In the case of traditional workers, their husbands also were engaged in traditional work (63.56%), and others were engaged in coolie work or other labours. None of them were engaged in modern occupation. Their education was also very low, when compared to those who were in modern occupation. In the case of daughters, they were highly educated, and their parents having modern occupation, did not like to do traditional occupation. Their parent's income was a major factor preventing them from doing traditional work.

Before we analyse the process of occupational mobility between two generations of Scheduled Caste women, we shall examine the nature of occupations in which the respondents are engaged in.

Regarding the nature of employment of the mother respondents, only a small percentage (0.88%) was in purely modern occupation. Among them, one mother was working as a teacher and the other was a superintendent. Majority (67.56%) of them were engaged in traditional occupation; 25.78 per cent were working as agricultural labourers, 2.22 per cent were other labourers and 3.56 per cent had no occupation and they were housewives.

3. V.S D'Souza, *Changing Socio-economic Conditions and Employment of Women in India,* in Transactional of the Indian Institute of Andvanced Study, Simla, Vol. 7, September, 1967, pp. 443-56.

In the case of the daughters, one third of them had no occupation. This is because, they were young and educated and they considered the traditional and casual occupation having low status. They did not like to do menial jobs. 32.89 per cent of daughters were still engaged in traditional work and 17.33 per cent were agricultural workers. 6.22 per cent were working as other labourers such as coolies, construction workers, loading labourers etc. Out of the remaining 23 daughters, 21 (91.30%) had white collar jobs and 2 (8.70%) had professional occupation.

The Scheduled Castes had their own traditional occupations in the past. The transition from traditional occupation to non-traditional occupation does not follow a uniform pattern. Today, they have many opportunities to play modern occupational roles. Among our mother respondents, only two had non-traditional occupation, the remaining were still engaged in traditional jobs (agriculture being included the traditional job). Eight mothers were not going out for work. Those who were in the traditional occupation were doing it for the last 11 to 20 years or more.

As against the mother respondents, only 32.88 per cent of their daughters were working in traditional jobs. One thing to point out is that both in the case of mothers and daughters those who were in traditional occupation were following it for the last so many years.

Inter-generational Occupational Mobility

In this study, we proceeded with the assumption that mothers' occupation was the starting point in women's inter-generational occupational mobility. In the case of women, it was seen that a daughter's occupational choice was most often influenced by her mothers' occupation. Here, we are trying to analyse the pattern of occupational mobility by examining the positions held by the mother respondents and daughter respondents. The following Table will make it clear.

TABLE 30

Inter-generational Occupational Mobility between Mothers and Daughters

Mothers' occupation	*Daughters occupation*						
	White collar	*Professional*	*Tradi-tional*	*Agri-culture*	*Other labourers*	*Unemployed*	*Total*
White collar	1 100.00%	—	—	—	—	—	1 0.44%
Professional	—	1 100.00%	—	—	—	—	1 0.44%
Traditional	12 7.89%	—	45 29.61%	21 13.82%	11 7.23%	63 41.45%	152 67.56%
Agriculture	4 6.91%	1 1.72%	27 46.55%	15 25.86%	3 5.17%	8 13.79%	58 25.78%
Other labourers	—	—	2 40.00%	3 60.00%	—	—	5 2.22%
Unemployed	4 50.00%	—	—	—	—	4 50.00%	8 3.56%
Total	21 9.33%	2 0.89%	74 32.90%	39 17.33%	14 6.22%	75 33.33%	225

The Table (Table No. 30) projects the process of occupational mobility between the mothers and the daughters. While 67.56 per cent of the elder generation was found to be engaged in traditional occupation, only 32.90 per cent of the daughters were in the traditional occupation. That is 35.32 per cent daughters had deviated from traditional occupation followed by their mothers. There was not a single daughter to be found who was in a lower occupational status than that of her mother who was in traditional occupation. Of the 67.56 per cent of mothers, only 29.61 per cent of their daughters were following the same occupation. The remaining 7.89 per cent were doing modern jobs in Government service. This could be considered as vertical mobility. Here we can see inter-generational vertical occupational mobility (upward), though only slightly. According to Theodore Caplow, "Vertical mobility is a movement of the individual upward or downward, with a gain or loss in social rank".[4] The simplest kind of vertical mobility is a change of occupation which involves a change in social position. In our study it was interesting to find that within the two generations of Scheduled Caste women at least at some had achieved positions higher than that of their mothers. The younger generation who were doing modern jobs had change in social status, remuneration, functions of work etc. Sorokin's explanation of vertical mobility can be applied here.

Intra generational mobility among the daughters was upward and vertical to some extent i.e. only 32 90 per cent were doing traditional work and the remaining 67.10 per cent had deviated to other jobs. Among them, 10.21 per cent had modern occupation, 17.33 per cent were doing agriculture work and 6.22 per cent were engaged in other works.

In the case of intra-generational occupational mobility within the mothers generation was horizontal. "Horizontal

4. Theodore Caplow, *The Sociology of Work*, McGraw Hill Book Company, New York, 1964; p. 59.

mobility is a change in function, including both technical and the social functions which arise from group membership. Horizontal mobility of the simplest type involves a change in employment within the same occupation." Among the mothers, 67.56 per cent of them were doing traditional occupation. 28.87 per cent of the remaining had deviated to other jobs. Among them, only 0.89 per cent had modern occupations, 25.78 per cent were doing agriculture work and 2.22 per cent were engaged in other works (The question was not relevant for 3.56 per cent who were unemployed). The other labourers and agricultural workers had no higher status or higher remuneration than traditional workers. Some of the respondents were doing work in Government services as scavengers which was also traditionally done by the Harijans. The only difference between the old and the new occupation was that in Government service the work was formal, regular and fetched a steady income. So these could be considered as horizontal mobility with some improvement in income. Hence, it can be proved that intra-generational mobility here was horizontal.

From this we can infer that intergenerational occupational mobility is vertical to some extent, intra-generational mobility among the daughters is to a small extent vertical, and intra-generational mobility among the mothers is only horizontal. These findings help up to prove our second hythothesis that though there was inter generational vertical occupational mobility, intra-generational mobility was horizontal.

Scheduled Caste Women in Traditional Occupation

Occupational Preference

From the analysis, it was found that traditional occupations were in the hands of the older generation, and non-traditional or modern occupations were in the hands of the younger generation.

While asking the mothers about their preference for occupation, it was found that 64.89 per cent preferred modern occupation to traditional occupation. Only 35.11 per cent preferred traditional occupation.

In the case of daughters, it was found that 90.67 per cent of them preferred modern occupation to traditional ones. This might be because, the younger generation preferred to do modern jobs that bring higher status and higher remuneration to them. But traditional work was casual and low paid and it offerred only a low status. Here, we observed the difference in the preference for modern occupation between two generations.

The following Table made clear the direction of change in the preference of occupation.

TABLE 31

Mothers' and Daughters' Preference for Occupation

	Preference in occupation		
	Mothers	*Daughters*	*Total*
Modern occupation	132 90.41%	14 9.59%	146 64.89%
Traditional occupation	72 91.14%	7 8.86%	79 35.11%
Total	204 90.67%	21 9.33%	225

Many sociologists have used occupation as a major indicator of social mobility of a caste. They had pointed out that the occupational desire of the mother determined the occupational desire of the daughter. This was true in the present study also. 64.89 per cent of the mother repondents preferred to do modern occupation while 90.41 per cent of their daughters preferred to do the some. While 35.11 per cent of mothers preferred to do traditional occupation, only 8.86 per cent of their daughters liked to do the same. It is clear here that those mothers who were worried about the low socio-economic status were anxious about their children's future and hence tried their maximum to provide education for them. As a result, 25.78 per cent of second generation deviated from the mother's opinion of preference for occupation. It was seen that more daughters desired to do modern occupation than traditional occupation.

Both the mothers' and daughters' data regarding the preference in occupation was analysed on the basis of their age, education, income, caste and district.

When the daughters data regarding preference for occupation was analysed using age as a variable, it was seen that cent per cent of the below 20 and 20—29 age groups preferred modern occupation. In the case of the 40—49 age group, 26.67 per cent liked traditional occupation and 35.29 per cent of above 50 age group, also liked the same. So it was clear that the lower the age, the greater would be their preference for modern occupation. Generally the older age group was not aware of the advantages of modern occupation and their low educational level would not help them to acquire modern occupation. So they wanted to stick on to their traditional jobs. The traditional jobs were less remunerative but it was only the means of their livelihood. So they took it for granted that they need not aspire for greater things. In addition to this, their strong belief that they are destined to perform traditional jobs only.

In the case of mothers it was observed that the younger age group preferred modern occupation to traditional occupation. In the below 40 age group. 75 per cent preferred modern occupation. At the same time only 61.90 per cent of the above 70 age group preferred the same. This may be due to the fact that, generally Scheduled Castes did menial jobs in the past and were condemned to having low status in the society. "The heirarchical occupational structure brings a low status to such occupations which are at the bottom".[5] Therefore, the younger generation did not want to do these stigmatic traditional occupations.

Education has relevance to the preference of occupation in the case of daughters and mothers.

As the educational level increased, the percentage of persons who preferred modern occupation also increased. It was observed that 46.15 per cent of the illiterates preferred to do traditional occupation. At the same time cent per cent of the

TABLE 32

Daughters' Education and Preference for Occupation

Daughters' education	*Preference in occupation*		
	Modern occupation	*Traditonal occupation*	*Total*
Illiterate	14 53.85%	12 46.15%	26 11.55%
Primary	9 69.23%	4 30.77%	13 5.78%
Upper Primary	25 83.33%	5 16.67%	30 13.33%
High School	60 100.00%	—	60 26.67%
S.S.L.C.	71 100.00%	—	71 31.56%
College	25 100.00%	—	25 11.11%
Total	204 90.97%	21 9.33%	225

5. Louis Dumont, *Home Hierarchies*, Vikas Publications, Bangalore, 1966, p. 103.

highly educated group i.e., the high school level and above educated preferred to do modern occupation. When compared to the educated respondents, only a small percentage of the repondents preferred modern job among the illiterates. The educated daughter respondents did not desire to do traditional job, because they considered traditional works to be inferior and low paid. It might be also due to the reason that higher education helped them to get modern occupation. This is clear from Table no. 32.

In the case of mothers, 44.76 per cent of illiterates and a small percentage of primary educated group preferred traditional occupation. In the case of higher educated group, cent per cent preferred modern occupation to traditional occupation. Educated people are aware of the benefits of modern occupation and they can very well aspire for modern occupation because of their education. It is clear from this study that as education of the respondent increased, the preference for modern occupation also increased. This supported the view that changes in occupation from traditional to non-traditional depend upon the levels of literacy,

It was clear from analysis that income of daughters influenced their preference for modern jobs. Cent per cent of the higher income group, (Rs. 301-400 to above 700) preferred to do modern occupation to traditional occupation. The higher income group was educated and they thought that modern occupation would fetch them high status in society.

In the case of mothers also the same trend was seen that lower income group preferred (61.54%) traditional occupation to modern occupation. This might be due to the fact that the lower income group was engaged in traditional occupation and they had only low level of education. They realised that modern education was essential for modern occupation. Since they were less qualified, they felt that they did not deserve it. This attitude made them think that traditional work was suitable for them. In the case of higher income group, cent per cent of them preferred modern occupation. It was also seen that in the Rs. 101-200 income group, 66.70 per cent preferred to do modern occupation; in the Rs. 201-300 income group 92.31 per cent also wanted to do the same. In the case of Rs. 301-400 and above Rs. 700 income group, cent per cent of them wanted to do modern occupation. As income increased, the number of respondents who preferred modern occupation also increased.

When we examined the relationship between place of residence (district as unit) and preference for occupation, it was found that among the daughters, a higher percentage of the respondents from Alleppey and Trivandrum desired to do modern occupation. As against the mother's view, their daughters' data from Palghat district proved that 81.33 per cent of them preferred to do modern occupation. It was due to the fact that the increasing awareness about the impact of modern education and occupation helped them to do for such jobs.

Districtwise analysis of mothers' data showed that 76 per cent of the respondents for Trivandrum and 84 per cent from Alleppey preferred modern occupation. But the majority of the respondents (65.33%) from Palghat preferred traditional occupation. This might be because of the higher rate of illiteracy of Palghat. Palghat is educationally backward and non-traditional or modern occupation required higher level of education. Traditional occupations of low status were found mostly among illiterates.

When asked about the reason for preferring modern occupation, both the mothers and daughters said that modern occupation had regular income and economic and social security which in turn contributed to high status in society.

"The status conferring function of occupation is of particular relevance in the case of Scheduled Castes. Occupying as they do, the lowest position in the caste hierarchy they were debarred from most occupations from time immemorial. Their caste position in traditional Hindu Society consigned them to certain defiling and polluting occupation which alone were open to them".[6]

When we asked the traditional workers whether there was any change in their working conditions from the past, 56.49 per cent of daughters who were engaged in traditional work, opined that there was change in the working conditions than in the past. Analysing the response of daughters we found that 47.24 per cent said that there was increase in salary, 37.01 per cent said that working conditions were better, 9.45 per cent said that there was better standard of living and 6.3) per cent said that there was change in status of work, than in the past.

Among the mother respondents, cent per cent of them opined that there was change in there working conditions than in the past. The question had relivance to 215 mothers only, because 8 mothers were not going outside for work and 2 had modern occupation. Among them, 45.58 per cent said that there were better conditions of work. 41.40 per cent said that there was better salary, 9.30 per cent said that there was status change, and 3.72 per cent spoke of the better standard of living such occupations offered. It was also found that 64.19 per cent of mother respondents had the idea of changing their jobs and gave the following reasons: insufficient salary (68.12%), lack of adjustment (15.22%) dislike for the present place of work (12.32%), and low status (4.35%).

Training in Traditional Occupation

With the objective of proving economic support to the Scheduled Castes, the State Harijan Welfare Department had established production-cum-training centres, in areas where Scheduled Caste population are highly concentrated. Vocational training was given in tailoring, basket and mat weaving,

6. C. Rajagopalan, *Op. cit.*, p. 149.

carpentary, rotten work and in traditional crafts like caragrass mat weaving, coir making etc.

The data about availing of training in crafts basket weaving, tailoring, cane work etc. showed that 15.52 per cent of daughter respondents had acquired the same. Of these 46 daughters, the majority belonged to Trivandrum and Alleppey districts. All of them got training from training centres run by the Harijan Welfare Department. It was seen that the scheme was not well known among the Scheduled Castes. None of the daughter respondents said that their children got training in such craft. Those respondent who had training, did not think it had helped them in earning a better livelihood. Their major complaint was that they were given training in their traditional jobs like cane work, basket making, weaving etc. which did not help them to get modern jobs. This was found to be true and the Government accordingly, has decided to implement a new employment programme for Scheduled Castes through these production-cum-training centres for training them in computer programming, two and three wheeler repair works, repair of electrical home appliances, plumbing, carpentary, tailoring and garment making, cosmetology etc.*

Participation in Unions

The Scheduled Castes as a whole, had ever been manual workers. But being a down-trodden class, they had been victims of exploitation for a very long time. The Gandhian movement had done a lot to make them aware that they too were human beings. At this stage, they had no political consciousness or awareness of their rights. It was with the emergence of the communist movement that they began to get organised on trade union or political lines. Alleppey was the first district where the communist party could organise Scheduled Caste

*Government of Kerala, Annual Administration Report, Scheduled Caste Development Deprtment, 1986-87.

agricultural labourers against the farmers. This resulted in their getting better wages and working conditions. "By and large, in areas where there are well organised trade unions, workers achieved higher wages, regulated hours of work, etc., as compared to the areas where they existed only in form."[7] More important was the development of a feeling that they should stand united to safeguard their interests. We can see the emergence of trade unionism here.

The Scheduled Castes have now become politically conscious and they are aware of their political rights and fight for their demands. Andre Beteille reports that "political participation creates normal atmosphere among the Harijans. It instills in them a new sense of confidence and raises high. their level of aspiration".[8]

All the mother respondents who were engaged in agricultural work had membership in six different unions. One of the reason for their taking membership in Union was for getting agricultural pension.

The six different Unions are :

(1) A.K.K.T.U. (All Kerala Karshaka Thozhilali Union),
(2) B.A.V.L. (Bharteeya Adhakrita Vaega League),
(3) K.S.K.T.F. (Kerala State Karshaka Thozhilali Federation),
(4) T.A.L.U. (Travancore Agriculture Labourers Union),
(5) C.I.T.U. (Centre of Indian Trade Unions),
(6) I.N.T.U.C. (Indian National Trade Union Congress).

Fifty per cent were having membership in A.K.K.T.U. and 20.93 per cent were members of B.A.V.L. and 20 per cent

7. A.M. Sharma, *Indian Journal of Social Work*, Book Review, 1980, Vol. XLI, No. 4, p. 417.
8. Andre Beteille, *Caste, Old and New*, Asia Publishing House, New Delhi, 1969, p. 100.

belonged to the K.S.K.T.F., 6.98 per cent were members of T.A.L.U., while 0.47 per cent were C.I.T.U. members, and 1.86 per cent were having membership in I.N.T.U.C. Even though they had membership in these Unions, all were not participating in their activities. Only 59.63 per cent had participation in the union activities. Mother respondents' participation in the union activities were not influenced by their age. But education seemed to have some influence. It was found that as education increased, the respondent's participation in union activities also increased. 53.15 per cent of illiterates had participation in union activities, whereas, cent per cent of SSLC had the same. The educated group had shown special interest in participating in union activities.

Irrespective of their age and education, cent per cent of the daughter respondents had membership in union and participated in the union activities.

All the respondents, both the mothers and the daughters, agreed that they enjoyed benefits due to membership in the union. They said that they got fixed wages, regulated hours of work, and above all, the unions induced them to fight for their rights.

Satisfaction with Present Job

It was found that the majority of our respondents from both the generations were not satisfied with their present jobs. Those who had no satisfaction were traditional workers.

In the case of daughter respondents, only 37.62 per cent were satisfied with their income and status and the remaining were not satisfied.

The younger age group was not satisfied with their income and status. As age increased, the satisfaction also increased. In the below 20 age group only 25.93 per cent were satisfied with their income and status. At the same time 60 per cent of the 50+ age group were also satisfied. This may be because the elder age group was only qualified for traditional occupation and they had to adjust with the income and status and hence had no frustration in that. The decrease in satisfaction among the younger age group indicated that a good number of them had no occupation. They were educated and were not going out for casual jobs. They have to depend upon their presents and felt disappointed in being a Scheduled Caste.

Among the mother respondents 19.74 per cent were satisfied with the present income and status and 80.26 per cent were not satisfied. The result of age-wise analysis showed that as age increased the dissatisfaction also increased. In the case of the above 70 age group 90.48 per cent were not satisfied with the same. It is interesting to note that 30 per cent of the younger age group were satisfied with their income and status, and only 9.52 per cent of the older age group were satisfied with the same. This may be because, the younger age group was more capable of doing work than the older age group. So the younger age group got work regularly which helped them to live happily. In the case of older age group they compared the present cost of living with that in the past. They complained that in the past, cost of living was very low and their wages were enough for better livelihood. So they expressed dissatisfaction in the present income and status.

Education of both the generations and satisfaction with income and status were found to be related. As education increased, satisfaction in income and status also increased. This increase came through education, since education was a status raising factor and helped to earn money through modern jobs. In the case of daughters 15.39 per cent of the illiterates were satisfied with their income and status, 87.50 per cent of the college educated were satisfied with the same. In general, we can say that, the educational level of a person determined his status. Higher the education higher will be his/her status in the society. Higher education will always fetch them more remunerative modern jobs. This can be the reason for their satisfaction.

Among the uneducated mother respondents, only 3.50 per cent were satisfied with their status and income. Those who were educated up to S.S.L.C., 75 per cent were satisfied with the same. In the case of the upper primary and above educated, the majority was satisfied with their income and status. In these groups, a few of them had government jobs such as scavengers and sweepers and had a regular income. So they were satisfied with their income and status. Even though they had traditional job, their status had improved since they were in government service.

The variables such as income and occupation were cross tabulated with the same response and it was found that the higher income group and a few traditional workers in both the generations were satisfied with their income and status. The higher income group included those people who had jobs in Government service. Among the daughter respondents 66.22 per cent of traditional workers were not satisfied with their income and status. This was because the majority of traditional workers were engaged in agriculture which was their traditional occupation. Agriculture work was seasonal and casual in nature. In the case of other labourers they got work more than the traditional workers and agricultural labourers. Among them, 50 per cent were satisfied with their income and status.

Occupation and Economic Status

The main function of an occupation is to fix a person to a social position with its consequent status and income. Various studies in general, demonstrated that occupational prestige, is highly correlated with income derived from occupation.

When the daughter respondents' economic status and occupation were analysed, it was found that among the below

Rs. 100 income group, the majority was traditional workers. The majority of Rs. 101-200 income group were those who had no occupation outside home. In the case of Rs. 201-500, the majority was traditional workers. The higher income groups were white collor workers and professional workers. This is because modern job fetch more money than the traditional work. Of the below Rs. 100 income group 76.92 per cent were doing traditional work. Of the total mother respondents, the majority belonged to Rs. 101 to Rs. 200 income group. Of these, 95 per cent were doing traditional work. The important thing to note here is that the white collar and professional workers carried high income.

Occupation and Social Status

"Status in the traditional Indian society was mainly determined by the institutions of family, and the caste, and in the changing society, other social institutions like education and also occupation emerge as the status determinants".[9] The Scheduled Castes know that they do not enjoy status in socity beause of their caste and occupation.

In the present study, an attempt was made to measure the respondents's opinion about whether traditional occupation was the main reason for their low status in society.

If the low-paid traditional jobs are the reason for the low status, improvement in the occupational pattern i.e., performance of modern occupational roles, will definitely contributes to the status improvement. In order to understand our respondents's reaction to this, we asked whether they thought that improvement in occupational pattern would help to release them from subservience to the higher castes. It was found that 59.56 per cent of daughers thought that it would help them. The remaining 40.44 per cent did not think so. This might be

9. S.K. Chauhan, *Op. cit*., (1980) pp. 154-55.

because they thought that they would not get anywhere near higher status, even though they acquired the same occupation as the higher castes did.

The same question was put to the mother respondents and it was found that 39.12 per cent of them thought that improvement in occupational pattern would help to release them from subservience, and 60.88 per cent did not think so. They opined

TABLE 33

Daughters' Age and Belief that Occupational Improvement Contributes to Higher Status

Daughters' Age	*Whether they think occupational improvement contributes to higher status*		
	Yes	*No*	*Total*
Below 20	48 84.21%	9 15.79%	57 25.33%
20—29	45 59.22%	31 40.78%	76 39.78%
30—39	23 51.11%	22 48.89%	45 20.00%
40—49	12 40.00%	18 60.00%	30 13.33%
50+	6 35.29%	11 64.71%	17 7.60%
Total	134 59.56%	91 40.44%	225

$X^2=28.81$
Degrees of freedom=4
Table value at .01 level=13.277
Contingency Coefficient=0.33

that even if they got modern jobs it was so on the basis of the principles of job reservation introduced by the government which in itself put the stamp of low caste on them. They had strong belief that they were subordinate class and deserved lower status. This belief was inculcated in them through the socialisation process. Their strong inferiority complex made them think that they would never get equal status with the high

TABLE 34

Mothers' Age and Belief that Occupational Improvement Contributes to Higher Status

Mothers' Age	*Whether they think Occuapational Improvement Contributing to Higher Status*		
	Yes	*No*	*Total*
Below 40	17	3	20
	85.00%	50.00%	8.89%
40—49	26	40	66
	39.40%	60.60%	29.33%
50—59	21	41	62
	33.87%	66.13%	27.56%
60—69	19	37	56
	33.93%	66.07%	24.89%
70+	5	16	21
	23.81%	76.19%	9.33%
Total	88	137	225
	39.12%	60.88%	

$X^2=31.5$

Degrees of freedom=4

Table value at .01 level=13.277

Contingency Coefficient=0.35

TABLE 35

Daughters' Education and Belief that Occupation Improvement Contributes to Higher Status

Daughters' Education	*Whether they think occupational improvement contributes to higher status*		
	Yes	*No*	*Total*
Illiterate	8 30.77%	18 69.23%	26 11.55%
Primary	4 30.77%	9 69.23%	13 5.78%
Upper Primary	10 33.33%	20 67.67%	30 13.33%
High School	24 40.00%	36 60.00%	60 26.67%
SSLC	32 45.07%	39 54.93%	71 31.56%
College	13 52.00%	12 48.00%	25 11.11%
Total	91 40.44%	134 59.56%	225

castes in society. These might prevent them from aspiring for modern jobs. These findings supported our third hypothesis that inferiority feelings still prevalent among those women contributed to their low rate of occupational mobility.

The data was analysed on the basis of age, education, income and occupation and was found to have relation.

It is clear from Table 33 that the younger age group thought that the improvement in occupational pattern would help them to get a release from the subservience to the higher castes. The majority of the below 40 age group had agreed to the statement at the same time, and among the above 50 age group, 35.29 per cent had agreed with that. From this it can be inferred that as age increased, the percentage of those who believe in the above fact decreased. This might be because that in a caste conscious society, the elder generation of Scheduled Caste had strong notion about casteism. They believed that only higher castes deserved higher occupation. Even if they succeeding getting higher occupation, this did not add to their status. Chi-square test supported the relationship between these two variables. (Chi-spuare test=28.81, Degrees of freedom 4, Table value at .01 level=13.277). Contingency coefficient of correlation O.33 also had shown significant relationship.

It was seen from Table 34 that the majority of the younger age group thought that the improvement in occupational pattern would help to release them from subservience to the higher castes. In the case of the above 70 age group, only 23.81 per cent had the same opinion. The older generation strongly believed that they would never get a chance to change their traditional occupations because of lack of modern education and hence could not change their traditional way of life and low status.

While only 30.77 per cent of the illiterates said 'Yes', 52 per cent of college educated said so. It was quite evident that as educational level increased, the respondents were more hopeful towards occupational improvement and better status. The majority of educated group thought that occupational change would help them to release them from subservience to the higher castes. At the same time, the illiterates had less faith in this.

It was obvious that the educated respondents expected improvement in occupational pattern to release them from subservience to the higher castes. The majority of mother respondents was illiterates and only a small percentage of the above 50 years age group had primary or middle school level of education. The educated group had the chance to mingle with the higher castes during their student life and were also aware of the advantages of education and its role in fetching modern jobs. Consequently, they strongly thought that by getting modern jobs they would improve their status in society and will change the attitude of the higher castes towards them. The variables such as income and occupation were also used for analysis. It was observed from mother respondents that in the lower income group, the majority (78.46%) did not think that improvement in occupational pattern would help to release them from subservience to the higher castes. This was because the lower income group was still engaged in traditional work and due to their lack of qualification there was no chance for improvement in their occupation. Daughter's data in this regard was found to have no significant relation.

On analysis using occupation as a variable on daughter respondents, it was found that cent per cent of the respondents in modern occupations thought positively. This may be because they had much experience in the work place, which in turn, gave them confidence.

Mothers' data also showed the same trend as the daughters'. Cent per cent of the white collar workers and professional workers had the opinion that improvement in occupational pattern would help to release them from sub servience to the higher castes. In the case of traditional workers and agricultural workers, the majority of them did not think so.

Scheduled Caste Women in Modern Occupation

As mentioned earlier, only 23 of the daughter respondents and 2 of the mother respondents were engaged in modern jobs. Though in the government service, has been reserved for the

Scheduled Castes, the actual percentage of them in employment is much less. Since the sample size was quite small, no tabulation had been done and statistical tests were also not applied.

In the case of daughters, 10 of them were Pulayas, 4 each were Mannas and Thandans, 2 each were Cheramars, and Kanakkans and 1 was Cheruman. 21 of them engaged in white collar jobs, and 2 were professional workers. white collars had passed SSLC, 7 had college education, and 2 of the professional workers were graduates. Among the Scheduled Castes, as the percentage of modern education increases, the opportunities for modern jobs and chances for vertical mobility have also increased.

Of the two mothers, one of them was working as superintendent and the other was a teacher. Both of them were having pre-university education, and were Pulayas.

When we enquired the reason for leaving traditional job, the daughters said that they were qualified for modern jobs, and traditional occupation was deagrding for them. In the case of mothers, one gave the reason of the traditional work having low status, and the other commented on its casual nature.

Taking into account the years of service, 2 daughter respondents had more than 11 years of service. In the case of the mother respondents, they had more than 20 years of service.

We enquird of both the mothers and the daughters about the number of their children working at present. In the case of the daughters, none of their daughters was working. The majority of daughters of the daughter respondents had not reached the age of government appointments. Some of them were highly educated and were frustrated because of not getting a job in the Government service. Being educated, they were against doing traditional jobs. Among the mother respondents, 3 of their daughters were in the Government service.

In chapter on 'Educational Mobility' it had been proved that the higher the education of the mother, the higher was the education of the daughter. Here also, a similar trend was observed, i.e., in the case of the mothers in modern occupation, their daughters were also having modern occupation.

Protective discrimination like reservation of posts for Scheduled Castes and Scheduled Tribes in Government services, relaxation of age limits, reduction in examination fees for entry into government services, and lowering down of educational qualification etc., have also been granted to the Scheduled Castes by the Government. Cent per cent of our respondents in modern occupation had availed themselves of the reservation of jobs. It may be due to the fact that they had secured jobs which were not warranted by their education, but through vacancies reserved for the Scheduled Castes.

When asked about the satisfaction regarding occupation, income and status, it was found that both mothers and daughters were satisfied then. In the case of status, the mothers were not satisfied, and 12 out of 23 daughters were also not satisfied. They also complained that their improved occupational, economic and social life had not received enough social recognition and hence were dissatisfied. A society where the caste distinctions is deep rooted may take more time to discard its differential treatment on the basis of caste. The respondents were asked whether they believed that by getting modern occupation. Scheduled Castes could improve caste status. Analysing the data of both the mothers and the daughters, it was found that cent per cent of them thought that modern occupation alone could not improve their caste status. They pointed out that even though economic improvement and better standard of living could fetch them friends from higher castes, it did not improve their caste status beyond a certain degree.

In the case of daughters, 39.13 per cent had the opinion that the improvement in their status was the consequence of modern occupation, for 39.13 per cant it was high income, and 21.74 per cent said that it helped them to get more social contacts which in turn would decrease social disabilities.

When asked whether they were free to use their income as they liked, it was found that 50 per cent of the mothers and 80.56 per cent of daughters said "Yes'. 50 per cent of mothers said that they hand over their salary to their husbands.

To find out whether these working women were consulted by their husbands in the decision making process in the family, their responses were analysed separately. 96.21 per cent of daughters were being consulted by their husbands in the decision making process in the family. In the case of mothers, only one was consulted by her husband in the decision making process.

Cent per cent of daughter respondents and mother respondents in modern occupation had savings.

As social status, to a greater extent, depends on the degree of participation in social activities, we asked our respondents about membership in cultural associations and the extent of their participation in them. It was found that cent per cent of daughter respondents, and 50 per cent of mother respondents had membership in associations like women's club, recreation club, etc. Only daughter respondents actively participated in their programmes.

When we take into account the intercaste relations, we found that the Scheduled Caste women in modern occupation enjoy a better status than their counterparts in traditional occupation, in the sense that all of them *had friends from* higher caste. They interdine with higher castes, visit higher caste's house regularly and also take part in the social functions of higher caste people. This proved that modern occupation has helped to a greater extent in discarding caste difference.

There was also noticeable change in the attitude of women in traditional and modern towards many common issues like dowry, age at marriage, endogamous marriage, divorce, family planning, equality for men and women etc. They were for higher age at marriage, for inter-caste marriage, against dowry, and cross-cousin marriage. They favoured family planning, widow remarriage and divorce, when it is absolutely necessary. These women in modern occupation strongly supported the view that men and women should given equal status in society.

These finding proved our fourth hypothesis that occupational improvement contributed to the social status of Scheduled Caste women.

Attitude Towards Children Following Traditional Occupation

One can make at least three arguments for including mother's occupation in a study of inter-generational occupational mobility. First the inclusion of this variable provides a better measure of family's socio-economic status, than father's occupation alone. Second, especially for women, mothers' occupation might represent and adult work-role model which affects the occupational choice of her children.[10]

When we asked the question to both the mothers and daughters whether they wanted their children to follow their traditional occupation, it was found that the daughter respondents' response was quite different from that of their mothers. Cent per cent of daughters said that they did not want their

10. Rachel A. Rosenfield, "Women's Inter-Generational Occupational Mobility", *American Sociological Review*, Vol. 43, 1978, p. 37.

children to follow the traditional job but to get modern jobs. They knew that the children had more opportunities for advancement in both education and job than they had. Besides, they were also of Government welfare measures and special programmes provided for them, which might help them to improve their socio-economic status.

In the case of mothers, 50.67 per cent were against their children following traditional occupation. The question was

TABLE 36

Mothers' Age and Attitude Towards Children following Traditional Occupation

Mothers' Age	*Attitudes Towards Children following Traditional Occupation*		
	Yes	*No*	*Total*
Below 40	2 10.00%	18 90.00%	20 8.89%
40—49	22 33.33%	44 66.67%	66 29.33%
50—59	34 56.67%	26 43.33%	60 27.56%
60—69	34 60.71%	22 39.29%	56 24.89%
70 and above	18 85.71%	3 14.29%	21 9.33%
Total	110 49.33%	113 50.67%	223

$X^2=34.43$
Table value at .01 level=13.277
Degrees of Freedom=4
Contingency Coefficient=0.36

put to all respondents who were engaged in traditional work and housewives who were not going outside to work. The data was analysed on the basis of variables such as age, education and occupation and was found to have relationship.

The majority of the mothers below 40 did not want their children to follow their traditioual work. In the case of the above 70 age group, 85.71 per cent of them preferred their children to follow traditional occupation. From this, we found that the older age group wanted to stick on to their tradition. So they ardently desired to do the traditional occupations and they preferred their children also to follow the same. They might not be aware of the advantages of modern jobs, especially when they were illiterates. Younger generation did not like their children to have job which perpetuated their low status. The X^2 test showed significant relation well beyond .01 level and coefficient of contingency (0.36) established this relationship.

Educationwise analysis showed that as education increased, the percentage of respondents who did not like their children to follow their traditional work also increased.

It was clear that among the illitrates, 46.85 per cent disliked their children following traditional occupation. At the same time, cent per cent of high school and above level educated mothers did not like their children to follow traditional occupation. Education had a prominent place in their conception about their children's occupation.

Another finding in this context was that mothers in traditional occupation (59.87%) wanted their children to follow traditional occupation. The remaining wanted their children to follow modern occupation. At the same time, none of the respondents who were not going outside for work disliked their children following traditional work.

When we examined the reason for their not willing to send their children for traditional work, they gave the following reasons.

The question was put to 202 daughters respondents and 223 mother respondents who were engaged in traditional jobs and who were not going outside for occupation. Among the daughters, 55.45 per cent gave the reason of traditional work having low status, 29.70 per cent gave the reason that traditional job fetched low income, 8.42 per cent opined that jobs of the kind were hard, and 6.44 per cent mentioned that that they were casual in nature.

Among the mothers, 46.02 per cent gave the reason as having low status, 36.28 per cent replied that brought low income, and 17.69 per cent pointed out the casual nature of work.

It was observed that the majority of mothers and daughters did not want their children to follow traditional work because of it's low status. Both the generations gave the second reason as low income involved in traditional work. Lower castes are more conscious of their status in the present times than in the early days and they appreciate the value of education and are trying to educate their children along with those of higher castes. Through education, they wanted to raise status by securing modern jobs. They also wanted to abandon their traditional work because of it's low income. This might be because traditional jobs fetch only less remuneration compared with modern jobs.

When we enquired the mother repondents as well as daughter respondents about the number of their daughters who, at present were engaged in modern jobs, it was found that among the mothers, 175 daughters were working, out of which 23(13.14%) were in modern occupation, 42.24 per cent were in traditional jobs, and 44.47 per cent were in other works. In the case of daughters, 57.15 per cent were in traditional work and 42.85 per cent were in modern jobs.

Hope for Better Occupational Prospects for Children

Let us now analyse the mother respondents' and daughter respondents' expectation of modern occupation for their children. It was found that 59.90 per cent of daughters and 50.22 per cent of mothers hoped for better jobs for their children. Parental pressure for higher education of children,

TABLE 37

Daughters' Age and Hope for Better Jobs for Their Children

Daughters' Age	*Hoping for better Job* *Yes*	*No*	*Total*
Below 20	41 75.93%	13 24.07%	54 26.73%
20—29	44 63.77%	25 36.23%	69 34.16%
30—39	20 50.00%	20 50.00%	40 19.80%
40—49	10 41.66%	14 58.34%	24 11.88%
50 and above	6 40.00%	9 60.00%	15 7.43%
Total	121 54.90%	81 40.10%	202

$X^2 = 13.44$

Degrees of freedom=4

Table value at .01 level=13.277

Contingency Coefficient=0.25

education opportunities provided by the Government for Scheduled Castes, job reservation, etc. were the reasons behind this hope.

The data was analysed on the basis of age and education and was found that younger age group hoped for better jobs than the older age group.

The majority (75.93%) of the younger age group hoped for better jobs for their children. At the same time, in the above 50 age group, 40 per cent had hope for better jobs for their children.

To find out the relation between age and response X^2 test was applied. It was found that there was relation between these two well beyond at .01 level. Contingency coefficient of correlation was also applied. We can infer from this that the younger age group preferred there children to go for non-traditional jobs due to the improvement in educational level and welfare measures. In the case of mothers also the same trend was seen.

As education increased the respondents' hope for better jobs for their children also increased. In the case of illiterate daughters only 33.77 per cent had hope for better jobs for their children. At the same time, 56.25 per cent among the college educated group had the same hope.

The majority of mothers with upper primary and above education hoped to get better jobs for children because of the better educational facilities available at present and also of the higher level of motivation to get status.

Table 38 shows that the younger generation hoped for better job for their children because of better motivation to get status. 46.34 per cent of below 20 age group hoped to get better job for their children due to motivation to get status. X^2

TABLE 38

Daughters' Age and Reasons for Hope for Better Job for their Children

Daughter's Age	*Hoping for better Job*				
	Better Educational Facilities	*More Encouragement for Parents*	*Better chance due to Reservation*	*Better Motivation to get Status*	*Total*
1	2	3	4	5	6
Below 20	6 14.63%	9 21.95%	7 17.07%	19 46.34%	41 33.88%
20—29	4 9.09%	11 25.00%	10 22.73%	19 43.18%	44 36.36%
30—39	2 10.00%	5 25.00%	8 40.00%	5 25.00%	20 16.53%

(*Contd.*)

1	2	3	4	5	6
40–49	1 10.00%	4 40.00%	1 10.00%	4 40.00%	10 8.27%
50 and above	1 16.67%	2 33.33%	1 16.67%	2 33.33%	6 4.96%
Total	14 11.57%	31 25.62%	27 22.31%	49 40.50%	121

$X^2 = 26.67$

Degree of freedom=12

Table value at .05 level=21.026

Contingency Coefficient=0.42

test showed the relation between these variables beyond the .05 level and the co-efficient of contingency correlation was 0.42.

Agewise and occupationwise analysis of mother's data did not show relationship. The daughter respondents' data was analysed with their occupation and found that 66.67 per cent respondents engaged in traditional occapation hoped to get better chance for job due to reservation and new job opportunities. In the case of agricultural workers, the majority was motivated in acquiring higher status.

Conclusion

The trend in occupational mobility among the two generarations of Scheduled Caste women showed that there was intergenerational occupational mobility. Among the mothers who were in traditional occupation (67.56%) only 29.61 per cent of their daughters were following the same occupation. The remaining 7.89 per cent were doing modern jobs in Government service. This could be considered as vertical occupational mobility. The younger generation who were doing modern jobs had change in social status, remuneration, and conditions of work. Here we can see inter-generational vertical occupational mobility.

In the case of intra-generational mobility, it was horizontal among the mothers and slightly vertical among the daughters. In the case of mothers, we found intra.generational horizontal occupational mobility because the agricultural workers and other labourers had no change in the status or higher remuneration. Among the daughter respondents we found that the daughters in modern jobs had change in social status, remuneration etc. So intra-generational mobility, among daughter respondents is vertical. These findings help us to prove our seconde hypothesis that though there was inter-generational vertical occupational mobility, intra-generational mobility was horizontal.

Since the occupational mobility is horizontal, except in the case of very few, the economic position of the respondents in the two generations was almost similar.

It was found that the younger age groups of both the generations preferred modern occupation. The variables such as income, educationtion and place of birth had relation with the preference in occupation. The higher educated and the higher income groups preferred modern jobs. A higher percentage of the respondents from Alleppey and Trivandrum desired to do modern occupation. The daughter respondents of Palghat district also preferred the same. Both the mothers and their daughters had the opinion that their working conditions had undergone change.

On the whole, it was found that 80.26 per cent of mothers, and 62.38 per cent of daughters were not satisfied with their jobs, because of the casual nature.

The majority of (60.88%) the mother respondents, and 40.44 per cent of daughter respondents thought that improvement in occupational pattern would not help to release them from subservience to the higher castes. Age, education, income and occupation were found to be related. As age increased the percentage of those who believed in casteism also increased. As educational level decreased, the respondents were less hopeful of occupational improvement. The lower income group and the respondents in traditional work also had less hope. Their strong inferiority complex made them think that they would never get equal status with high castes in society. These might prevent them from aspiring for modern jobs. These findings supported our third hypothesis that inferiority feelings still prevalant among the Scheduled Caste women prevent their educational attainment and consequently contributed to their low rate of occupational mobility.

In the case of mothers in modern occupation, their daughters were also having modern occupation. Ii was found that both the mother respondents and daughter respondents were satisfied with their income and occupation. In the case of status, both the generations were not satisfied. They also told that modern occupation could not improve their caste status. They also pointed out that modern occupation helped to get more social contacts, which in turn, would decrease social disabilities.

The respondents in modern occupation enjoyed higher status. They had more freedom of movement, had role in decision making process, had freedom to spend money and also they had membership and participation in cultural activities. They were having contacts with higher caste people and their attitudinal difference was also remarkable.

These findings proved our fourth hypothesis that occupational improvement contributed to the social status of Scheduled Caste women.

In the case of the attitude of the mothers towards their childrens 'occupation, 50.67 per cent wished to get higer occupation than they had. The older generation, the lower income group, and the illiterates wanted to stick on to their traditional jobs. Both the mothers and their daughters gave reason for their unwillingness to send children for traditional work as it was of low status. They were, however, hopeful of getting new occupations with better remuneration.

CHAPTER V

Cultural Mobility

Culture, in its broadest sense, denotes "the totality of learned behaviour transmitted from one generation to another".[1] Cultural mobility, for the purpose of our study, refers to change among the two generations of Scheduled Caste women in areas such as intercaste relations; practice of untouchability; marriage and family; religious beliefs and customs; food habits and dresses and political participation.

Inter-Caste Relations

According to Prabhu the low rank of the Harijans resulted from cumulative, inequalities in the economic and political and ritual system".[2]

With the increase in education, more Scheduled Castes were in favour of breaking the taboos on intercaste relationship

1. Ralph L. Beals, (et. al.), *An Introduction to Anthropology*, Mac Millan Publishing Co., New York, 1971, p. 704.
2. P.N. Prabhu, *Report of the Seminar on Casteism and Removal of Untouchability*, Published by Indian Conference of Social Work, Bombay, 1955, p. 104.

through interdining, social visits etc. Now the conditions have changed and Scheduled Castes are treated at par with higher castes.

For understanding the pattern of interpersonal relationships between Scheduled Castes and upper castes, we asked the respondents about the habit of visiting the houses of upper castes. The majority (70.22%) of mother respondents said that 15 years ago they never visited the houses of the higher caste, and the rest told us that they visited rarely. When we analysed the present situation, we found that 4 per cent of the mother respondents visited the higher castes regularly and 37.33 per cent frequently, 45.33 per cent rarely visited, while 37.33 per cent never visited the higher castes. 15 years ago, none of the mother respondents visited higher caste's houses regularly or frequently. But in these days, 27.33 per cent of them frequently visited higher caste's homes. It is interesting to note that before 15 years 70.22 per cent of the mothers never visited the higher castes. But today only 13.33 per cent said that they never visited higher caste' houses. 37.33 per cent told us that they frequently visited the higher castes. We can see the change within the same generation in the caste society.

The same question was put to the daughter respondents and it was found that 41.33 per cent of them visited frequently, another 41.33 per cent of them visited regularly and only 17.33 per cent of them visited rarely. The Table 39 shows the pattern of visiting the houses of the higher castes by the two generations.

It was found that 4 per cent of the mother respondents and 41.33 per cent of the daughters had the habit of visiting the higher castes reqularly. It was interesting to note that when 13.34 per cent of mothers told us that they had never visited the higher castes, none of their daughters said the same. These differences seem to indicate mobility between the two generations.

An analysis of the factors responsible for this mobility is relevant. The daughters habit of visiting the higher castes's houses and their age were found to have significant relationship.

TABLE 39

Mother's and Daughters' Habit of Visiting Higher Caste's Houses

Nature of visit	*Mothers'*	*Daughters'*	*Total*
Regularly	9 4.00%	93 41.33%	102 22.67%
Frequently	84 37.33%	93 41.33%	177 39.33%
Rarely	102 45.33%	39 17.34%	141 31.33%
Never	30 13.34%	—	30 6.67%
Total	225 100.00%	225 100.00%	450

The Table 40 reveals that as age increased the tendency of the daughter respondents to have more contact with higher castes decreased. Among the below 20 age group, 50.88 per cent of them visited the higher castes regularly. This may be because of the younger people's educational status i.e., they got more chance to make company with the higher caste friends in the schools and colleges. In the case of the above 50 age group, 29.41 per cent revealed that they regularly visited the higher castes' houses. Here we found vast difference between the younger age group and the older age group. X^2 test and contingency coefficient were aplied to this data and was found to have significant relationship (X^2=48.35, degrees of freedom 8.

TABLE 40

Daughter's Age and Visiting Higher Castes

Daughter's age	*Visiting Habits*			
	Regularly	*Frequently*	*Rarely*	*Total*
Below 20	29 50.87%	24 42.11%	4 7.02%	57 25.33%
20—29	32 42.10%	36 47.37%	8 10.53%	76 33.78%
30—39	17 37.78%	19 42.22%	9 20.00%	45 20.00%
40—49	10 33.33%	12 40.00%	8 26.67%	30 13.33%
50+	5 29.41%	2 11.77%	10 58.82%	17 7.56%
Total	93 41.33%	93 41.33%	39 17.33%	225

$X^2=48.35$

Degrees of Freedom=8

Table value at .01 level=20.090

Contingency Coefficient=0.42

Table value at '01 level =20.090. Contingency coefficient of correlation is 0.42).

Taking into account the mother's age, it was found to influence the habit of visiting the higher caste's house i.e., as age increased the habit of visiting the higher castes decreased.

Among the below 40 age group, only 35 per cent of them had never visited the higher caste houses, at the same time 90.48 per cent of the above 70 age group never visited the higher castes. This may be because of the untouchability which was prevalent 15 years age and none of the higher castes allowed the lower castes to visit their houses.

Daughter's education also influenced their habit of visiting higher castes' house. The following Table gives the results.

TABLE 41

Daughters' Education and Visiting Friends of Higher Castes

Daughters' education	*Visiting Habits*			
	Regularely	*Frequently*	*Rarely*	*Total*
Illiterate	1 3.85%	9 34.62%	16 61.53%	26 11.55%
Primary	1 7.69%	6 46.15%	6 46.15%	13 5.78%
Upper Primary	9 30.00%	13 43.33%	8 26.67%	30 13.33%
High School	27 45.00%	29 48.33%	4 6.67%	60 26.66%
S.S.L.C.	35 49.30%	31 43.33%	5 7.04%	71 31.56%
College	20 80.00%	5 20.00%	—	25 11.11%
Total	93 41.33%	93 41.33%	39 17.33%	225

The above Table shows the difference between the interaction and the social contact of the educated and the illiterate Scheduled Caste women with higher caste people. 80 per cent of the college educated daughter respondents said that they visited the higher caste's houses regularly. At the same time only, 3.85 per cent of the illiterate respondents visited the higher castes regularly.

Analysis of mother's data shows a very significant relationship between education and their habit of vistting the higher castes. Nobody from the illiterates and less educated respondents, i.e., those who had below high school level education, visited regularly, the higher caste's house. In the case of the high school educated mothers, 50 per cent of them visited regularly and cent per cent of the SSLC and college educated respondents also did the same. Here we can draw the inference that the higher level of education increased their contacts with the higher castes. Education was the factor which was responsible for minimising the intensity of pollution. It also helped them to strengthen the social exposure with high castes. The educated Scheduled Caste people would thus get more chance to mingle freely with the high castes.

A significant change in social position of the Scheduled Castes was the reduction in caste restrictions due to two factors. One of them was anti-untouchability laws and another was education of Harijans. Education is the only medium which made them conscious of their privileges. This decrease in caste restriction has been evident in many forms.

On our enquiry, it was found that there was much difference between the two generations in the case of having higher caste friends. The following Table will make it clear.

The younger generation had more high caste friends than the elder generation. It was found that the majority (66.22%) of mother respondents had none of the high caste friend. Only

TABLE 42

Mothers' and Daughters' having Higher Caste Friends

Having Higher Ceste Friends	*Mothers'*	*Daughters'*	*Total*
None	149 66.22%	32 14.22%	181 40.22%
A few	76 33.78%	82 36.44%	158 35.11%
A lot	—	111 49.33%	111 24.66%
Total	225 100.00%	225 100.00%	450

33.78 per cent of them said that they had a few friends from higher castes. As far as daughters were concerned, it was found that 49.33 per cent had a good number of higher caste friends and 36.44 per cent had a few, and only 14.22 per cent opined that they had no friends from higher castes. This change between the generations showed the reduction in social distance.

The data was analysed on the basis of age, education, income and occupation.

As age increased, the friendship with the high caste decreased. The Table 43 strengthened the view to a great extent i.e. 7.80 per cent of the 20-29 age group told us that they had no higher caste friends. 53 per cent of the above 50 age group also said so. The X^2 test showed a significant relation well beyond .01 level and the coefficient of contingency (0.34) showed that there was correlation between between the two.

TABLE 43

Daughters' Age and Having Higher Caste Friends

Daughters' age	*Having Higher Caste Friends*			
	None	*A few*	*A lot*	*Total*
Below 20	—	17 29.82%	40 70.18%	57 25.33%
20—29	6 7.89%	30 39.48%	40 52.63%	76 33.78%
30—39	8 17.77%	17 73.38%	20 44.44%	45 20.00%
40—49	9 30.00%	12 40.00%	9 30.00%	30 13.33%
50+	9 52.94%	6 32.29%	2 11.77%	17 7.50%
Total	32 14.22%	82 37.44%	111 49.33%	225

$X^2 = 29.47$
Degree of Freedom=8
Table value at .01 level=20.090
Contingency Coefficient=0.34

In the case of the mothers also this was found to be true. Higher the age, lesser the number of friends from the higher castes. 25 per cent among the below 40 age group, and 66.67 per cent of the above 70 age group had no friends from the higher castes. This difference makes it clear that age has considerable influence on friendship between the high castes and the Scheduled Castes. The older age group had a feeling that since they were Scheduled Caste people, they were denied of the contact with the other higher castes. Belng Scheduled Castes, they had faith on caste restrictions. Once educated, they move around freely, meeting people casting aside the caste prejudices. "In a developing country, like India, the education system has become a powerful instrument of economic and social changes for accelerating the process of transforming it's traditional agrarian ways and means of living into those of a modern and industrial society."[3]

Education is a conservative force, and as such it assimilates, the culture, customs, and beliefs and transmits them from one

TABLE 44

Daughters' Education and Having Higher Caste Friends

Daughters' Education	*Having High Caste Friends*			
	None	*A few*	*A lot*	*Total*
Illiterate	13 50.00%	10 38.46%	3 11.54%	26 63.55%
Primary	5 38.46%	5 38.46%	3 23.08%	13 5.78%
Upper Primary	9 30.00%	25 40.00%	9 30.00%	60 13.33%
High School	5 8.33%	25 41.67%	30 50.00%	60 26.67%
S.S.L.C.	—	23 32.39%	48 67.61%	71 31.56%
College	—	7 28.00%	18 72.00%	25 11.11%
Total	32 14.22%	82 36.44%	111 49.33%	225

3. Vimal P. Shah, Tara Patel and William H. Shewell, Sociological Bulletin. Journal of Indian Sociological Society (Gujarat and Wisconsin Universities), Vol. XX, No. 2, Sept. 1971, p. 113.

generation to the other. In the case of the daughters, education always seemed to be an important factor contributing to social contacts with higher caste friends.

It is seen from Table 44 that the high school and above educated group had more friends from the high castes. While only 11.54 per cent of the illiterate daughter respondents had higher caste fricnds, 50 per cent high school educated, 67.61 per cent SSLC educated, and 72 per cent of college educated had the same. There is none omong thc daughter respondents with higher educatiou without high caste friends.

In the case of mothers, a good majority (79.02%) of illiterates had no friendship with high castes. In all cases, cent per cent of the persons with the higher education had a few high caste friends. Here it seems to have a vast difference among illiterates, lower educated and higher educated.

Occupationwise analysis of daughter's data proved that the respondents in traditional occupation have less friends with high castes, compared with those having modern occupation. The majority of agricultural workers had a number of high caste friends. Those having modern occupation, because of their higher education could easily mingle with others. But in the case of traditional workers, they had their own complexes.

The same trend was seen in the case of mothers also. The cent per cent of the mothers in modern occupation had friendship with higher castes. 65.52 per cent of agricultural workers also said that they had friendship with high castes. This may be because the agricultural labourers had close contact with the land owners who belong to the high caste.

The respondents who did not have high caste friends had their own reasons for that. Of the mothers who were without higher caste friends, 43.11 per cent said that they thought that friendship with high castes was not proper. This may be because of their inferiority complex that they belonged to lower caste. 14.22 per cent of them complained that high castes did not admit them to their houses. 8.89 per cent noted that elder members in higher castes family did not like their visits. 56.25 per cent of the daughter respondents also voiced first reason that was given by the mothers.

Another way to analyse the inter-group participation was ask the respondents to furnish the details of being invited for social functions along with higher castes. It was found that 28 per cent of the daughter respondents never participated. 23.33 per cent expressed that they rarely participated in such functions, and 48.67 per cent said that often they attended.

Cent per cent of the mother respondents voiced that in former days, they never participated in the social functions which the higher caste people attended. But today the condition has changed. 48 per cent of the mother respondents said that they rarely participated and 11.33 per cent said that often they did and 5.67 per cent said very often. Only 35 per cent said that in the present time also they never participated in the social functions where high caste attended.

For analysing the intercaste relationship, the respondents were asked to state whether they thought it was prestigious to have high caste people visiting their houses. 42.22 per cent of daughter respondents thought it was prestigious, while cent per cent of the respondents belonging to the older generation thought so. The older generation was more affected by the restrictions and disabilities of the lower castes than the younger generation. For them it is prestigious to have high caste friends visiting them.

The daughters' data was analysed on the basis of age and education and it was obvious that as age increased, the percentage of those who believed that the visit of higher castes was prestigious, also increased. But education was not found to have significant relationship.

TABLE 45

Daughters' Age and Visit of Higher Caste People as Prestigious

Daughters' age	*Whether it is prestigious to have Highre Caste Peoples Visit*		
	Yes	*No*	*Total*
Below 20	12 21.05%	45 78.95%	57 25.33%
20—29	29 38.16%	47 61.84%	76 33.33%
30—39	25 55.56%	20 44.44%	45 20.00%
40—49	17 56.66%	13 43.33%	30 13.33%
50+	12 70.59%	5 29.41%	17 7.50%
Total	95 42.22%	130 57.78%	225

$X^2=22.45$
Degrees of Freedom=4
Table value at .01 level=13.277
Contingency of Coefficient=0.30

It is clear that 21.05 per cent of the below 20 age group thought that it was prestigious. In the case of 50+ age group, 70.59 per cent of them also thought on the same lines. Today, there are governmental and legal aids and almost equal opportunities for education and occupation which should be helpful for social advancement.

The respondents were asked to state whether they used caste with their names. In the course of discussions with the respondents, some of them said that they did not like to use their caste names because if they did, others would look upon them as inferiors. In traditional society, their ancestors were known with caste names, such as Neeli Pulayi, Chatan Pulaya. Today they do not like to reveal their caste identity with their names. They also agreed that compared to the earlier times, the status of Scheduled Castes have improved a great deal.

In our study, when we asked them on what account did they think that the other castes discriminate against Scheduled Castes, our respondents opined that it was on account of the economic discrimination. They said that if a person was wealthy, the qustion of his caste was insignificant. Both the younger and the elder generation supported the statement that economic independence would minimise caste discrimination.

Practice of Untouchability

"Untouchability is intimately and organically associated with the institution of caste. It's rigid form is a logical outcome of the deliberate creation of a peculiar notion of pollution sactified by religious and codified by the Brahminical laws. This helped the institutionalisation of caste hierarchy and untouchability and gave them both a socio-religious approval."[4]

The majority (65.78%) of our daughter respondents never suffered from untouchability and 25.33 per cent suffered occasionally, and 8.89 per cent suffered quite often. In the case of mothers, 87.56 per cent of them said that they suffered from it very often and 12.44 per cent suffered occasionally.

4. Venkata Retnam, *Social Mobility of Scheduled Castes in Madhurai*, Project Report, I.C.S.S.R., p. 8.

TABLE 46

Mothers' and Daughters' Suffering from Untouchability

Suffering from Untouchability	*Mothers'*	*Daughters'*	*Total*
Very often	197 87.56%	20 8.89%	217 48.22%
Occasionally	28 12.44%	57 25.33%	85 18.88%
Never	—	148 65.78%	148 32.88%
Total	225 100.00%	225 100.00%	450

From the above Table it is clear that three-fourth of the mother respondents had suffered from untouchability very often while only one-tenth of their daughters had the same experince.

Often it is said that educational advancement and economic development of Scheduled Castes will automatically erase untouchability. In our study the educationwise analysis of daughters' data did not show any relationship, while mother's data showed significant relationship. It can be seen that 97.40 per cent of the illiterate mothers had very often suffered untouchability. At the same time, 33.33 per cent of the high school educated and 25 per cent of SSLC educated suffered the same. It is clear that education is an instrument in minimising social disabilities.

Inter-dining with Forward Castes

With the impact of modern education, Scheduled Castes were in favour of breaking the taboos on inter-caste relationship in inter-dining, social visits, etc. Educated people always will get chance for close contact with higher castes, thereby reducing the social distance.

89.78 per cent of daughters had never dared to dine with higher castes, some fifteen years back. Educationwise analysis shows that in earlier days none of the illiterate or the primary educated respondents dined with them. 84 per cent of college educated also never dined with them. Here we can see the intensity of social distance prevalent among lower castes. In those days even educated Scheduled Castes people were not treated as equals by high castes. In the case of mothers, none were invited to dine with higher castes when they visited them.

With the impact of modern education, and debarring of untouchability, more Scheduled Caste women are invited to dine with higher caste hosts. The percentage of inter-dining increases with the increase of education. In both the mothers' and daughters' cases, the above fact was found to be true.

It was found that 50.67 per cent of daughters had dined with high castes while visiting them. In the case of mothers, 92 per cent of them said that they wrre not invited to dine with higher castes. Education is the most important factor contributing to the change in inter-dining of Scheduled Castes and Higher Castes. The Table 47 proves this.

Majority of the illiterates (69.23%) were never invited to dine with high caste while visiting them, while 76 per cent of college educated said that they were invited to do so. As education increased, interdining also increased.

The analysis also revealed that none of the illiterates and primary educated mothers were invited to dine with high castes. The upper primary and above educated group were invited to do so.

When asked whether any high caste friends took part in Scheduled Caste's social functions, it was seen in present times,

TABLE 47

Daughters' Education and Interdining with Higher Caste

Education	*Inter-dining with Higher Caste*		
	Yes	*No*	*Total*
Illiterate	8(30.77%)	18(69.23%)	26(11.55%)
Primary	4(30.77%)	9(69.23%)	13(5.78%)
Upper primary	14(46.67%)	16(53.33%)	30(13.33%)
High school	30(50.00%)	30(50.00%)	60(26.67%)
SSLC	39(54.92%)	32(45.08%)	71(31.56%)
College	19(76.00%)	6(24.00%)	25(11.11%)
Total	114(50.67%)	111(48.33%)	225

higher caste friends participated in their social functions. All the mother and daughter respondents said that often they had guests from higher castes for their social functions.

In early days, there were restrictions on food among castes. It was found that 52 per cent of the daughter respondents said ther give cooked food to higher castes in their family. In the case of mothers, 31.11 per cent also said 'Yes'. These respondents were highly educated i.e., high school and above level. The people who said they gave cooked food to high castes meant that the higher castes took part only in tea party, when there were some functions like marriage etc. They also revealed that most often high caste people were ready to take food from their house, if it was cooked by high caste people. The mother respondents still believed that it was not proper to give food to higher castes prepared by them, because they were untouchables. They also added that the high castes would not like their preparation.

Caste Organisations

In earlier times, there were caste panchayats. The caste panchayat among the Scheduled Castes was not well organised, and that was why people usually said that there was no caste panchayat among Scheduled Castes. However, they existed all the same and settled all matters related to marriage, divorce, and other ritual and social affairs important for Scheduled Castes. Caste based organisations began to appear towards the end of the 19th and early 20th centuries. Scheduled Caste leaders also began to form associations to speak up for their caste group for special demands and treatment from the government.

In our study, 39.11 per cent of the mother respondents and 80.89 per cent of the daughters had membership in caste organisation. There was considerable difference between these two generations. This may be because of the absence of such organisations during the early period. It was also pointed out by some mothers that due to illiteracy they were not aware of the advantage of caste organisations. Another reason was that caste organisations were more prominent and active in certain districts like Trivandrum and Alleppey only. While cent per cent of the daughter respondents from Alleppey district had membership in caste organisation, 84 per cent of respondent from Trivandrum also had the same. The lowest percentage of membership in caste organisation were in Palghat.

In the case of mothers, Trivandrum had the highest percentage (49.33%) of membership in caste organisation. In Palghat district, only 26.67 per cent had membership which being the lowest rank in order. This might be due to the fact that Palghat was educationally backward and consequently they were not having much idea about caste organisation and its advantages.

Most of the caste organisations in which the mothers and daughters had membership had similar functions. While 55.88 per cent of the daughter respondents had membership in Kerala Pulaya Maha Sabha, only 2.21 per cent had membership in Sambava Maha Sabha.

The mothers had membership in caste organisation like Kerala Pulaya Maha Sabha (54.55%). Kerala Cherumar Maha Sabha (7.95%) Bharateeya Adhakritha Varga League (22.73%), Kerala Sambava Maha Sabha (2.27%), Kerala Manner Maha Sabha (9.09%), and Kerala Thandar Maha Sabha (3.41%).

The four functions of caste organisations are educational, social, recreational and settlement of disputes. The education of the caste organisation means providing financial assistance and free tuition for those who are economically handicapped. Caste organisation also rewards the bright students of their community with cash or some prizes.

During the time of marriage, the bridge and bridegroom should sign on a register book which is specially made for marriage registration. The couples should pay Rs. 30/- for registration, and the organisation gives a marriage certificate. The President or the Secretary will give some gifts to the couples in the name of caste organisation on the marriage day. The gift will be some times in cach or in kind. If there is any conflict between the couples, the caste organisation will interfere and help them to arrive at a compromise, or in unavoidable cases, the organisation will make arrangement for divorce.

At the time of death the organisation gives Rs. 101 for the expenses of cremation. The amount will be enhanced if the family is economically handicapped. In some places, there are reading rooms and Mahila Samajams for women and children. In Trivendrum district, in Venganoor, there is Mahila Samajam and Nursery School functioning under Kerala Pulaya Maha Sabha.

Marriage and Family

Each caste has it's own customary rules and regulations governing marriage. It may also be subjected to regulation by a religious body. The basic features of marriage is companionship, satisfaction of sexual instinct, procreation and economic partnership. The process of industrialisation, urbanisation and secularisation have brought about social psychological change in the attitudes and values held by people towards marriage and family.

In order to study the process of changing pattern of marriage, the respondents's age at the time of marriage, attitude towards intercaste marriage, dowry system, widow remarriage, divorce, and marital adjustment, were taken into account.

Age at Marriage

"Among the Scheduled Castes there is no fixed age for marriage. Early marriage is very common among them. According to their belief when a girl attains puberty ; she becomes polluted. So the girl should be married before this when she is still unpolluted".[5]

"Child marriages were common upto 1931. Owing to the effort of social reformers, Child Marriage Restraint Act was passed in 1929. It came into force from 1931. According to this Act, conducting marriage of a female child under 14 years of age and a male under 18 is punishable. With the enforcement of Child Marrige Restraint Act of 1929. also known as Sharda Act, helped a lot to minimise early marriages.

As a result of higher education, better employment opportunities and the breakdown of joint family system, there is a tendency to raise age at marriage.

Among the daughter respondents 116 were married and 109 were unmarried. 42.24 per cent were married at the age of 15 or below, and 24.13 per cent were married between 16—20

5. L.P. Vidyarthi, *Op. cit.*, pp. 209-210.

years and 19.83 per cent were married between 21—26 years and 13.79 per cent were married above 27 years.

While analysing the age at marriage of mother's generation, it was found that 56.14 per cent of them were married off at the age of 15 or below, 39.55 per cent were married between 16-20, 2.67 per cent were married between 21—26 and 0.44 per cent after 27. Two mothers were not able to recall their age at marriage.

The following Table shows the rate of mobility in age at marriage of daughters and mothers.

TABLE 48

Age at Marriage Among Daughters and Mothers

Age at Marriage	*Daughters*	*Mothers*	*Total*
15 and below 15	127(56.44%)	49(42.24%)	176(51.61%)
10-20	89(39.55%)	28(24.13%)	117(34.31%)
21-26	6(2.67%)	23(19.83%)	29(8.50%)
Above 26	1(0.44%)	16(13.79%)	17(4.99%)
Not applicable*	2(0.88%)	—	2(0.59%)
Total	225(100%)	116(100%)	341

*Not able to give the age at marriage.

The Table made clear the difference in age at marriage of the two generations. The rise in age at marriage is clearly pronounced in the case of daughters. Among mothers, 0.44 per cent had married at the age of above 26, while among the daughters it is 13.79 per cent. But at the lowest age at marriage there is not much difference. But this supports the fact that early marriage is still prevalent among the Scheduled Castes.

The daughter's data shows remarkable influence of education on age at marriage.

It is clear from the table 49 that 39.13 per cent of the illiterate daughter respondents were married at the age of 15 or below. In the case of college educated group 75 per cent of them were married at the age of 26 and above. We can infer from this Table that education had an influence on one's age at marriage. This may be because education helped an individual to act purposively. The educated persons knew the drawbacks of early marriage and they wanted to marry only after full development of the self. Postponement of marriage would offer better opportunities for women to improve their education, economic status, and promote social change and get relief from traditional bondage.

The mother's data was analysed on the basis of educational level of the respondents. It was found that higher the education, higher was their age at marriage. It was interesting to note that when 64.34 per cent of illiterate mothers had married at the age of below 15, nobody who had high school and above education married at the same age. 25 per cent of SSLC educated group had married at the age of above 26. Higher education contributes to postponement of marriage.

Preferred Age at Marriage for Children

Next we shall see the difference of opinion about age at marriage of sons between two generations.

It could be seen from the table 50 that 40.89 per cent of mothers preferred the marriageable age for their sons to be between 25 and 27. In thc case of daughers, 41.78 per cent preferred their sons to marry at the age between 28 and 30. Here we can see the difference of preferred age at marriage i.e., younger generation preferred late marriage for their children. It was assumed that the educated respondents would prefer higher age at marriage for their children ; both boys and girls, compared to less educated respondents.

TABLE 49

Daughters' Education and Age at Marriage

Daughters' education	*Daughters' Education*				
	Below 15	*16-20*	*21-25*	*26 and Above*	*Total*
1	2	3	4	5	6
Illiterate	9 (39.36%)	8 (34.78%)	3 (13.04%)	3 (13.04%)	23 (19.83%)
Primary	4 (36.63%)	5 (45.46%)	2 (18.18%)	—	11 (9.48%)
Upper primary	9 (40.91%)	3 (13.64%)	6 (27.27%)	4 (18.18%)	22 (18.97%)
High School	14 (51.85%)	2 (7.41%)	3 (11.11%)	8 (29.63%)	27 (23.28%)

(*Contd.*)

1	2	3	4	5	6
SSLC	4 (16.85%)	6 (24.00%)	5 (20.00%)	10 (40.00%)	25 (21.55%)
College	—	—	2 (25.00%)	6 (75.00%)	8 (6.86%)
Total	40 (34.48%)	24 (20.69%)	21 (18.10%)	31 (26.76%)	116

TABLE 50

Mothers' and Daughters' Preferred Age at Marriage for Sons

Preferred Age at Marriage	*Mothers'*	*Daughters'*	*Total*
Below 25	47 20.89%	61 27.11%	108 24.00%
25—27	92 40.89%	70 31.11%	162 36.00%
28—30	86 38.22%	94 41.78%	180 40.00%
Total	225 100.00%	225 100.00%	450

A greater percentage among the illiterates and primary, and upper primary educated respondents preferred early marriage for boys, whereas in the next three educational categories i.e., High School, SSIC and college educated, the majority considered 28 to 30 years as the proper age. This may be because the educated people knew the value of education and they wanted to educate their children. Also they liked see their children getting married after securing some jobs.

Agewise analysis of both mothers and daughters shows that as age increased the preference of early marriage also increased. The majority (64.19%) of below 20 age group preferred their sons to marry between 28-30 years of age. At the same time, among the above 50 age group the the majority (88.23 %) wanted to get their sons married at the age of below 25. The younger age group preferred late marriage because they wanted their sons to complete their higher education and to acquire a job before getting married to enable them to overcome economic difficulties. Age had a considerable influence on preference for sons' age at marriage among the mother respondents. Younger generation did not favour early marriage even for their boys. This may be because the older age groups were most probably illiterates and they did not know the draw backs of early marriage. Among the younger generation, 85 per cent of them considered 28 to 30 years as ideal age for their sons to get married.

Preferred Age at Marriage for Girls

Information was also obtained regarding the opinion of the mother respondents and the daughter respondents about the proper age at marriage for girls. It was assumed that the elder generation would prefer a lower age at marriage for their daughthers when compared to the youger generation. The level of education of a respondent was considered likely to help determining the age at marriage for their daughters. The

TABLE 51

Mothers' and Daughters' Preferred Age at Marriage for Girls

Preferred Age at Marriage	*Mothers'*	*Daughter's*	*Total*
Below 15	6 2.67%	—	6 1.33%
15—18	36 16.00%	77 34.22%	113 25.11%
19—22	126 56.00%	39 17.33%	165 36.67%
23—26	57 25.33%	109 48.45%	166 36.89%
Total	225 100.00%	225 100.00%	450

opinion of the mothers and the daughters regarding preferred age at marriage for girls, was analysed and found to have difference of opinion. The Table 51 makes the difference clear.

While analysing the rate of mobility, it was found that none of the daughter respondents considered the proper age for marriage for girls was below 15. At the same time, a small percentage of mother respondents considered so. 48.45 per cent of daughters preferred the age between 23 to 26 for girls.

It is clear that only 10.53 per cent of the below 20 age group thought 15-18 years as the appropriate age for girls to marry. At the same time, 88.24 per cent of the above 50 age group also thought in the same manner. X^2 text also showed significant relation well beyond .01 level and contingency coefficient (0.52) showed there was correlation between the two.

Among the mother respondents below 40 age group, 50 per cent preferred their girls to be married at the age of 23-26 years. At the same time, nobody from the above 70 age group thought so. 19.05 per cent of the same group preferred the girls to be married off at the age of below 15 years. This might be because elder generation considered that girls should marry as early as possible after they become mature, Another reason was that in earlier days child marriages were prevalent and they still insisted on that type of marriage.

The Table 52 indicates that a greater percentege among the illiterates and primary educated respondents preferred 15-18 years, as the proper age at marriage for girls, whereas out of the other three categories i.e. high school, SSLC and college level educated, a majority preferred 23-26 to be the proper age. Here education seemed to be a significant factor in people's opinion about the marriageable age of girls. As age increased the preferred age at marriage for girls also increased. The X^2 test showed significant relation well beyond ·01 level and coefficient of contingency (0.40%) showed there was correlation between the two.

TABLE 52

Daughters' Education and Preferred Age at Marriage for Girls

Daughters' Education	*Preferred Age at Marriage* 15—18	19—22	23—26	*Total*
Illiterate	14 53.85%	9 34.62%	3 11.54%	26 11.55%
Primary	7 53.85%	4 30.77%	2 15.39%	13 5.78%
Upper Primary	15 50.00%	7 23.33%	8 26.67%	30 13.33%
High School	21 35.00%	6 10.00%	33 55.00%	60 26.67%
S.S.L.C.	14 19.72%	11 15.49%	46 64.79%	71 31.56%
College	6 24.00%	2 8.00%	17 68.00%	25 11.11%
Total	77 34.22%	39 17.33%	109 48.45%	225

$X^2=40.34$
Degrees of freedom—10
Table value at .01 level=23.207
Contingency coefficient=0.39

Mothers' education-wise analysis showed that educated respondents preferred higher age at marriage for their girls. The majority of (64.34%) illiterate respondents regarded the age of 19-22 years being appropriate for their daughters. At the same time, 83.33 per cent of the high school educated and cent per cent of the SSLC and the college educated considered the age of 23-26 years as appropriate.

Attitude Towards Endogamous Marriage

Traditional Hindu marriages follow a number of prohibitions and considerations for selection of partners. Along with the endogamous and exogamous restrictions, much emphasis is laid in the personal qualities and characteristics of the perspective bride and bridegroom. Moreover, the social, economic and clan status of the respective families are taken into consideration.

As regards endogamy, it was desired that the varna of the husband and wife should be the same, hence savarna marriages were prescribed. Endogamy is characteristic of caste system.

When asked about endogamous marriage, it was found that 89.78 per cent of daughters and 94.22 per cent of mothers insisted on an endogamous marriage. Both the generations gave the following reason for their insistance. 42.26 per cent of daughters opined that the treatment of spouse would be different, and 30.38 per cent said that marriage bond would not last, and the remaining 27.36 per cent gave the reason that the members of their families did not allow intercaste marriages. They desired to marry with the the consent and co-operation of their parents. In the case of mothers, majority (50.26%) gave the reason that the treatment of the spouse would be different, 35.38 per cent said that marriage bond would not last, and only 14.36 per cent opined that the members of their families did not allow intercaste marriages.

The attitude of the mother's and the daughters' regarding the insistance on endogamous marriage showed only slight difference. The reason for this difference of opinion might be because caste feeling was still strong among Scheduled Castes.

The younger age group had much chance of mingling with higher castes and they did not want to insist on endogamy.

TABLE 53

Mothers' and Daughters' Attitude Towards Endogamy

Attitude Towards Endogamy	*Mothers'*	*Daughter's*	*Total*
Yes	212 49.22%	202 89.78%	414 92.00%
No	13 5.78%	23 10.22%	36 8.00%
Total	225 100.00%	225 100.00%	450

Modern education also had considerable influence regarding the opinion about insistance on endogamous marriage. In the case of daughters, education did not have much influence.

Educationwise analysis of the mothers's data showed that as education increased the tendency to insist on endogamous marriage decreased. 97.90 per cent of illiterate mothers insisted on endogamous marriage, at the same time 80 per cent of the college educated group said that they did not want to insist on the same. One respondent who had college education had intercaste marriage; her husband belonged to a higher caste. Educalion, thus, had a negative effect on endogamous marriage.

Attitude Towards Intercaste Marriage

Hindu sub-castes are strictly endogamous. Marrying a person from outside one's own caste is intercaste marriage. Due to the adherence of caste system there were only few instances of inter-caste marriages in villages, in early period. With the advent of modern education, the caste barriers began to disappear and there emerged a favourable attitude towards marriages. Inter-caste marriages have been legalized by the Hindu Marriage Act of 1955. The government also encouraged such marriages by providing many benefits including financial help.

C.T. Kannan's comparative study obout inter-racial marriages in London shows that "intellectual affinity, educational and vocational similarity, common attitudes and temperaments, at times opposite and complementary traits, economic necessity and various other social and personal factors have influenced the spouses come together and unite in marriage.'[6]

"In recent years, due to the spread of education, the attitude of the people seems to have changed to some extent and there is a considerable relaxation of caste restriction on matrimonial relationship."[7] Moreover, legal act also considers intercaste marriages to be valid. Naturally educated people want to marry educated spouses only. In lower castes, the educated have not been able to find suitable spouse from their own castes.

Keeping these facts in view, in the present investigation an effort had been made to study the attitude of Scheduled Caste women on this issue. Only 14.22 per cent of the mothers and 22.66 per cent of the daughters approved of intercaste marriage. This indicates that Scheduled Caste women were more conservative and they wanted to stick on to endogamous marriage. The Table 54 will make clear the difference in attitude of mothers and daughters towards intercaste marriage.

The slight difference in attitude towards the intercaste marriage of mothers and daughters proved that they were

6. C.T. Kannan. *Interracial Marriage in London*, S.W. (Litho) Printers Ltd., London, 1972, p. 127.
7. Abha Avasthi, *Hindu Marriage in Continuity and Change*, Lucknow Publishing House, Lucknow, N.D. pp. 119-20.

TABLE 54

Mothers' and Daughters' Attitude Towards Intercaste Marriage

Attitude Towards Intercaste Marriage	*Mothers'*	*Daughters'*	*Total*
Approve	32 14.22%	51 22.66%	83 18.44%
Disapprove	193 85.78%	174 77.34%	367 81.56%
Total	225 100.00%	225 100.00%	450

conscious of their low caste position and believed that marriage alliance with a higher caste was not advisable. In the present study, only one mother respondent had intercaste marriage, and her husband belonged to a high caste. The parents and relatives of the husband had not given their consent for the marriage. Even now there is no contact between both the families.

In the case of daughters, no intercaste marriage had taken place. The variables such as age and education were found to influence the attitude of mothers towards intercaste marriage and among daughters only age had any influence.

The daughter respondents' age-wise analysis showed that in the younger age group (below 20) 15.79 per cent strongly approved of intercaste marriage and in the above 50 age group, only 5.88 per cent strongly approved of the same.

45 per cent of mothers in the below 40 age group strongly approved of the intercaste marriage, at the same time in the above 70 age group, only 4.75 per cent approved of the same.

The educationwise analysis of mothers' data showed that as education increased the attitude towards intercaste marriage became favourable. Only 2.10 per cent of the illiterate respondents strongly approved of intercaste marriage and 25 per cent of the SSLC educated and 50 per cent of the college educated strongly approved of the same. The educated people seemed to have a favourable attitude towards intercaste marriage.

The attitude and practice of intercaste marriage among Scheduled Caste women proved that there was uot much mobility in the case of marriage.

When asked whether they thought that they could improve caste status by inter-caste marriage, only 7.11 per cent of the daughter respondents strongly agreed that by intercaste marriage they could improve caste status and 44.89 per cent of them disagreed with this. In the case of mothers, none of them

TABLE 55

Mother's and Daughters' Opinion about Caste Status and Inter-caste Marriage

Thinking Intercaste Marriage can Impr.ve Status	*Mothers'*	*Daughters'*	*Total*
Strongly Agree	—	16 7.11%	16 3.56%
Agree	7 3.11%	47 20.89%	54 12.00%
Disagree	29 12.89%	61 27.11%	90 20.00%
Strongly Disagree	189 84.00%	101 44.89%	290 64.44%
Total	225 100.00%	225 100.00%	450

strongly agreed with this. Only 3.11 per cent of them agreed and 84 per cent of them strongly disagreed.

Table 55 makes clear that the older generation strictly opposed intercaste mariage. At the same time, 20.89 per cent of the daughter respondents also thought so. This might be due to the fact that the younger generation had more education and contact with other high castes, which in turn, would contribute to their attitudes and beliefs.

Attitude Towards Cross Cousin Marrigae

In traditional Indian society, cross-cousin marriages were approved. But today such marriages are rare. Keeping in mind the fact that the educated respondents were exposed to eucation and had ideologies and attitudes towards cross cousin marriage, it was assumed that educated people had unfavourable attitude towards the same.

When asked about their attitude towards cross cousin marriage, it was found that 82.22 per cent of the mothers desired that, whereas only 31.11 per cent of the daughters respondents agreed to it.

TABLE 56

Attitude Towards Cross-Cousin Marriage : Mothers' and Daughtees'

Attitude	*Mothers'*	*Daughters'*	*Total*
Desirable	185 82.22%	70 31.11%	225 56.66%
Undesirable	40 17.78%	155 68.89%	195 43.34%
Total	225 100%	225 100.00%	450

The data was analysed on the basis of age, education and it it was found there was significant relation. An agewise analysis of both the generations reveaved that as age increased, the attitude towards cross cousin marriage also changed. In the case of daughters among those who were below 20, 14.03 per cent said it was desirable and 85.97 per cent of them said it was undesirable. As in the case of the above 50 age group, the majority (52.94%) preferred cross cousin marriage. The reason for change in attitude of the younger age group might be the influence of education and modernisation.

While 50 per cent of the younger age group showed an unfavourable attitude, only 19.05 per cent of the elder generation had the same view. Here we found a vast difference between these two age groups, the younger age group was aware of the draw backs of cross cousin marriage. Some of them said that it would lead to hereditary diseases. Some said it would create family problems. But the older age group preferred it because they wanted to strengthen there relation with their relatives through cross-cousin marriages.

In the case of both the generations, education had a great influence on their attitudes.

From Table 57 it is clear that the illiterate respondents were having more favourable attitude towards crross-cousin marriage. But the highly educated group (high school and above) had a less favourable attitude towards the same. As education increased, the attitude towards cross-cousin marriage also changed. Today, the younger generation realises the disadvantage of cross-cousin marriage like lack of adjustment within the members of the family, the conflicts in families etc.

X^2 test was also applied and showed significant relationship well beyond at .01 level (contingency correlation was also found to have relation).

TABLE 57

Daughters' Education and Attitude Towards Cross-cousin Marriage

Daughters' Education	*Attitude Towards Cross-cousin Marriage*		
	Desirable	*Undesirable*	*Total*
Illiterate	14 53.85%	12 46.15%	26 11.55%
Primary	7 53.85%	6 46.15%	13 5.78%
Upper Primary	12 40.00%	18 60.00%	30 13.33%
High School	17 28.33%	43 71.67%	60 26.67%
S.S.L.C.	15 21.13%	56 78.87%	71 31.56%
College	5 20.00%	20 80.00%	25 11.11%
Total	70 31.11%	155 68.%89	225

X^2=21.22
Degrees of freedom=5
Table value at .01 level=15.086
Contingency Coefficient=0.29

While 90.91 per cent of the illiterate mothers said cross-cousin marriage was desirable, only 33.33 per cent of the high school educated and 25 per cent of the SSLC educated group said so. It is surprising that none of the college educated supported the same. It is evident that as educational level of the respondent increased, the number of respondents who were

TABLE 58

Mothers' Education and Attitude Towards Cross-cousin Marriage

Mothers' education	*Attitude Towards Cross-cousin Marriage*		
	Desirable	*Undesirable*	*Total*
Illiterate	130 90.91%	13 9.09%	143 63.56%
Primary	41 77.35%	12 22.64%	53 23.56%
Upper Primary	11 64.71%	6 35.29%	17 7.56%
High School	2 33.33%	4 66.67%	6 2.67%
S.S.L.C.	1 25.00%	3 75.00%	4 1.77%
College	—	2 100.00%	2 0.88%
Total	185 82.22%	40 17.78%	225

against cross-cousin marriage also increased. Thus education had a positive effect on Scheduled Caste women to feel that cross-cousin marriage was undesirable,

Attitude Toward Arranged Marriage

"In the traditional joint family, parents were morally obliged to find mates for their children and the children were expected to accept the choice. As marriage was looked upon as an agreement between two young people, love was not a necessary element as a basis for selection, nor was courtship a necessary prelude for testing the relationship".[8]

An attempt has been made to analyse the change in attitude towards arranged marriages. For obtaining information on this aspect the question was asked "Who will arrange the marriage of your children ?". The following Table will make clear the difference of attitudes between two generations.

TABLE 59

Mothers' and Daughters' Attitude Towards Arranged Marriage

Attituae Towards Arranged Marriage	*Mother's*	*Daughter's*	*Total*
Parents will Arranged	155 68.88%	134 59.56%	289 64.22%
Approve the Selection of their Children	70 31.12%	91 40.44%	161 35.78%
Total	225 100.00%	225 100.00%	450

It is seen from the above Table that 68.88 per cent of the mothers said that parents would arrange marriage for their children, and the rest of them would approve of the selection made by their children. In the case of daughters, 59.56 per cent said that they would first consult with their chidren and then would take a final decision. The remaining 40.44 per cent opined that parents would arrange marriage for their children. Those respondents who were not in favonr of arranged marriage were having modern education and belonged to younger age group.

8. D. Ross Ailen, *Hindu Family in its Urban Setting,* University of Toronto, Toronto Press, 1961.

Attitude Towards Divorce and Widow Remarriage

In all communities, one major factor which affects the status of women is the practice for divorce. In the words of Kapadia, "dominion of the man over his wife is further asserted by the fact that he is permitted to divorce his wife at his own pleasure and without justifying his action".[9] Divorce asserted man's domination over his wife and lowered her position.

The traditional belief of marriage as a sacrement and an indissoluable union, did not allow divorce. But the early Hindu Law permitted remarriage for men. The remove this injustice, divorce was legally sanctioned to women.

In our study all the respondents said that their family allowed divorce and they thought that divorce laws which also give women the freedom to divorce are necessary for improving the status of women.

In the early period, women were not permitted to remarry. After the reform movement, Widow Remarriage Act of 1856 came into existence which permitted women to remarry. Among the lower castes, the widows could and did enioy the previlege of remarriage which was not the case among the high castes of the Hindu society. In our study 86.74 per cent of mothers and cent per cent of daughters preferred widow remarriage, and said that their family permitted it.

Attitude Towards Dowry System

"In India in the lower strata, it is customary for the women to work in gainful occupations, therefore women are an economic asset to the family, whereas in the higher strata, they are regarded as an economic liability because they are not bread winners. Therefore, in the lower sections when a daughter is married, it means the loss of a productive worker, in otherwords, an economic loss to the parents of the

9. K.M. Kapadia, *Marriage and Family in India*, Indian Branch, Oxford University Press, London, 1958, p. 113.

girl. Thus, in many cases the loss is compensated by a 'bridge price', Bridge price may be described as the customary amount that is paid for the bride at marriage".[10]

Baddhyopadhyaya had noted that "the dowry system in the sense of something already promised was probably not very common, although references to the gift of large sums of money and valuable presents along with the daughters are noticed in our literary and epigraphic records".[11]

Generally, the conditions changed and dowry came into existence and had become a common practice among almost all the communities in modern society. Though dowry system originated as a part of the religious custom, in course of time, it took an ugly turn and began to create serious problems in the 20th century. A dowry is a sum of money or property that is brought to the marriage by the girl.

Both the generations in our study said that dowry was undesireable. This might be because of the fact that the bulk of the members of Scheduled Castes were still engaged in low paid traditional jobs which yielded only low income. They were not in a position to pay dowry. Our data showed that the custom of dowry was prevalent among Scheduled Castes. Out of the 116 daughters who were married, 72(62.07%) had given dowry. In the case of mothers, 49.78 per cent gave dowry. The following comparative analysis showed difference of dowry payment within two generations.

Here we found variation in payment of dowry between two generations.

10, M.N. Srinivas, *Marriage and Family in Mysore*, New Book Co., 1942, p. 14.

11. Samaresh Bandhyopadhyaya, *Foreign Accounts of Marriage in Ancient India*, Firma K.L. Mukhopadhyaya, Calcutta, 1973, p. 34.

TABLE 60

Mothers' and Daughters' Payment of Dowry

Payment of Dowry	*Mothers'*	*Daughters'*	*Total*
Yes	112 49.78%	72 62.07%	184 53.96%
No	113 50.22%	44 37.03%	157 46.04%
Total	225 100.00%	116 100.00%	341

The data was analysed on the basis of age and education. In the case of daughters, none of them was found to be related Mother's age and payment of dowry were found to be related. As age increased, the payment of dowry decreased. In the age group below 40, 70 per cent of the mother respondents had paid dowry at the time of their marriages, at the same time only 19.05 per cent of the above 70 age group paid the same. This gives ample proof that in earlier days, there was no practice of dowry among the Scheduled Castes.

Family

Many of the customs of Scheduled Castes regarding marriage are also undergoing change. One of the important changes is that marriages are conducted in public places, and temples. in olden days it was not possible because of caste discrimination. In general, the customs of Scheduled Castes are fading fast since they are considered outdated by the younsters. This may be because of modern education, urbanisation and improvement in economic condition.

In any society family is a social organisation and it is the most outstanding primary group. The role of women in society is still defined largely in their functions as wife and mother.

"Family's socialisation function and its various structural forms played vital role in the process of social mobility, because it reaches the child first and has greatest influence on his or her aspirations, motivations and early training."[12] The quality and size of the family may throw some light on the features of social and economic life of a community.

Type of Family

There are two types of family seen in Kerala, i.e., joint and family nuclear family. Rarely we can see extended family. Joint family consists of a number of married couples and their children who live together in the same house. In all societies the independent nuclear family is common.

In our study we found two types of families such as extended and nuclear. In the case of mother respondents, 50.22 per cent were found living in nuclear family, and 37.33 per cent in extended family. The modern trend was thus towards nuclear family.

Attitude Towards Joint Family System

While asking the opinion about the joint family system, the respondents pointed out its disadvantages rather than the advantages. Both the younger and the elder generations preferred nuclear family. The advantages of joint family system according to them were :

(1) it gave social security for elder members,

(2) it minimised economic burden, and

(3) more income could be collected through all the members of the family.

The disadvantages pointed out were the following. the head of the family. In their opinion in a joint family had more

12. Savitha Mehra, *Social Mobility in Rural Haryana*, University of Hissar, Ph.D. Thesis, 1982, p. 78.

responsibility. There was no freedom to express their own opinions. Joint family system created conflict between the younger generation and the elder generation. Lack of adjustment would affect the happiness of the whole family. It also led to economic strains to the household. Our respondents' comments about the joint family system showed that they especially the daughters, were well informed about its advantages and disadvantages.

Attitude and Practice of Family Planning

In our study, the lowest number of members in family was 2—4 and the highest 8—10. The mother's generation has got larger family size.

An examination of the attitude of respondents towards family planning showed that among the daughter respondents, cent per cent of them showed favourable attitude. In the case of mothers, 53.33 per cent had favourable attitude towards family planning. The mother's data was analysed with the variables, and was found that with the increase in age their attitude was less favourable. As age increased, the percentage of women who favoured family planning decreased. Among the below 40 age group, 80 per cent showed favourable attitude towards family planning and 14.29 per cent of 70+ age group preferred the same. This might be because the younger age groups were aware of the advantage of birth control. And the older age group had some religious beliefs about pregnancy and child birth. Education had considerable influence on attitude towards family planning. 50.35 per cent of illiterate respondents had unfavourable attitude towards family planning, and 33.33 per cent of the high school educated had the same. None of the SSLC and the college educated group had unfavourable attitude. All of them showed favourabld attitude This might be due to the fact that educated did not find any thing wrong in limiting the number of children. With the increase of education more Scheduled Caste women were in favour of family planning.

In contrast to the favourable attitude towards family planning, it was found that only 7.56 per cent of the mother respondents practiced the same. In the case of the higher age group, most of them passed menopause and the question was not applicable to them. During their time, the family planning programmes were not very popular and the common people were not aware of the advantages of birth control. Moreover, elderly people considered it a sin to control birth artificially.

In the case of daughter respondents, 70 (60.34%) had practiced family planning. The youngest age group (below 20) were recently married and that may be the reason for not practising family planning. The people who had practiced family planning were highly educated and belonaed to the middle income group.

In Mehra's opinion, low percentage of practice of family planning among untouchables might be due to their low level of education, or due to economic factors".[13] In their study, in the case of mother respondents those who practiced family planning had less education, as in the case of daughter respondents. 70 per cent of them had high school education and 30 per cent had college education. Here our study establishes close relation between education and practice of family planning.

18.67 per cent of the mother respondents considered 2—3 children and 21.33 per cent of them desired to have 4—5 and the majority (60%) prefarred more than 5 children as the ideal number. In the case of daughter respondents, majority (62.67%) preferred less than 2 children ; 19.56 per cent preferred 2—3 and 15.11 per cent preferred 4—5 and only 3.67 per cent preferred more than 5. The following Table will make clear the difference between the mothers' and the daughters' opinion regarding the same.

13. *Ibid.*, p. 58.

TABLE 61

Opinion of Mothers' and Daughters' about the Ideal Number of Children a Couple should have

Number of children	*Mothers' Opinion*	*Daughters' Opinion*	*Total*
Less than 2	—	141 (62.60%)	141 (31.33%)
2—3	42 (18.67%)	44 (19.56%)	86 (19.11%)
4—5	48 (21.33%)	34 (15.11%)	82 (18.22%)
More than 5	135 (60.00%)	6 (2.67%)	141 (31.33%)
Total	225 (100%)	225 (100%)	450

The diference of opinion between the two generations was high. This may be due to the fact that the younger generation were aware that when number of children decreased, it would help parents to bring them up properly and to provide them with all facilities.

Preference to Male Child

"The lingering hang over of joint family structure, and the dependence on sons to provide social security in old age, keep the desire to have a son in Indian families. While a girl is considered an economic liability, a son is considered as an economic asset, a social grace and religious redeemer. While a son may be expected to carry on the family line or prestige forward, the girl is held in trust by her parents on behalf of her future in laws."[14]

14. Augustine S. John. The Indian Family in Transition. Vikas Publishing House, New Delhi, 1982, p. 43.

When we asked whether they preferred male child, 86.67 per cent of the mothers and 61.78 per cent of the daughters preferred boys. Between these two generations, we found slight difference of preference. The following Table will make it clear.

TABLE 62

Mothers' and Daughters' Preference to Male Child

Preference to male child	*Mothers'*	*Daughters'*	*Total*
Yes	195 86.67%	139 61.78%	334 74.22%
No	30 13.33%	86 38.22%	116 25.78%
Total	225 100.00%	225 100.00%	450

This change might be due to the impact of modern education on the younger generation. The educated mothers thought that it made no difference whether they were boys or girls, provided they were given good education and reared properly.

The respondents who preferred male child did so since they thought that the boys would look after the family. Once married, the girls would not be able to help their parents.

Decision-making in the Family

Having a major role in decision making process in the family is an indicator of women's status. "Women in a family often enjoy a position of subordination and thus act as junior partners of men. Seniority in age or in generational status may give a women a higher symbolic rank in relation to certain men in the family, but generally male superiority in the Hindu family is supported by tradition and man's rights of property."[15]

We tried to find out whether Scheduled Caste women had freedom to express their views in decision making in the family. In the case of married daughter respondents, 48.27 per cent got chance sometimes, 35.35 per cent said that they got chance for expressing their views 'always' and only 19 (16.38%) never got any chance for expressing their views. As far as their mothers were concerned, 60.87 per cent of them got chance 'sometimes' and 31.56 per cent never got it, Only 7.56 per cent 'always' felt free. The following Table will make clear the rate of mobility within two generations.

TABLE 63

Rate of Mobility in Decision Making in the Family

Decision making in the family	*Mothers'*	*Daughters'*	*Total*
Always	17 7.56%	41 35.35%	58 17.00%
Sometimes	137 60.87%	56 48.27%	193 56.60%
Never	71 31.57%	19 16.38%	90 26.39%
Total	225 100%	216 100%	341

It is evident from this Table that the elder generation had lesser role in family decision making than the younger generation. The younger generation had significant role in

15. M.S. Gore, Urbanisation and Family Change, Popular Prakashan, Bombay, 1968, p. 156.

decision making. This might be because of their education, which gave them confidence.

The data was analysed on the basis of age and it was found that age and decision making in the family were related. Educationwise analysis showed no relationship. As age increased, the freedom to express views decreased. Among the below 20 age group 37.5 per cent said that they had freedom to express their views always, at the same time only 12.50 per cent of the above 50 age group had the same. In the case of respondents who never got chance for expressing their views freely were only 12.5 per cent of the below 20 age group and 56.25 per cent of the above 50 agc group. Here we found a vast difference between these groups. This might be because while comparing to early days Scheduled Caste women were more educated now. So they could easily understand the problems and among these groups couples had mutual understanding about their family problems, and they jointly tried to find solution for the same. This would lead them to express their views frankly.

In the case of mother respondents also as age increased, the freedom to express views in the family decreased.

Religious Belief and Customs

Religion is an institution which helps to maintain peace of mind by regulating relation between man and the God. In traditional Hindu society Scheduled Castes were the most degraded sections of the society. So Scheduled Castes associated themselves with their own religions and had their own modes of worship. They had their own temples and deities, rituals, and festivals and also had their own priests. Their Gods and Goddesses were different from that of high castes. Each caste has its own deities. The most important among them are Chathan, Mootha Chathan, Madan, Marutha, Porutty, Cherutty, Kali, and Thampuran. In some places like Palghat, Pulayas and Kanakhans even now practice ancestor worship. Deceased ancestors were propitiated by offering toddy, chicken blood etc. In Palghat every house had 'Altharas' (a small platform made of mud) for worshipping their deities. During festivals like Thiruvathira, Onam, etc. they make offering to their deities as part of celebrating the festivals. Their priests are known as "piniyals" and they offer prayers and sacrifices.

There is considerable change in the traditional religious beliefs, customs and rituals of Scheduled Castes. To find out these changes within the two generations, we collected data of the same. From the analysis, it was found that both the morhers and daughters had belief in God.

When we asked whether they worshipped separate deities it was found that 62.22 per cent of daughters worshipped their own caste deities, and 80.89 per cent of the mothers also did the same. The older generation, even at present, believed in their own deities such as Chathan, Porutty, Cherutty etc. But the younger generation said that they had belief in Gods of Hindu pantheon like Shiva, and Aiyappa. The data was analysed on the basis of place of birth, age, education, occupation and income. In these variables area and age was found to have relation.

As the age increased, the pattern of worshipping separate deities also increased. This is especially true in the case of the younger age group who had to go outside for work. Among the daughter respondent 26.32 per cent of below 20 age group were worshipping separate deities and 88.24 per cent of 50+ age group also did the same.

The analysis of the mothers' data also showed the same trend. Among the group below 40, 65 per cent were worshipping deities and in 60-69 and the above 70 age group. 83.93 per cent and cent per cent respectively were worshipping their own deities. The caste restrictions on religion and worship were prevalent in the days of the older respondents. Cosequently they were forced to worship their own separate deities.

Majority of both the generations worshipped at home. Only in Trivandrum and Alleppey the respondents worshipped at religious institutions.

Visits to Temples

The data regarding visits to temples reveals that 34 per cent of daughters and 60 per cent of mothers visited the temple. Only 13 per cent of the daughters and 22 per cent of the mothers visited the temples regularly. This might be because the older generation got enough time for visiting temples. The younger age group usually would not pay more attention to worshipping or visiting temple. They had to involve in matters relating to their families. In household matters, older people would pay less care when compared to the younger people. It was found that most of the Scheduled Castes had made considerable headway in the observance of upper caste Hindu religious beliefs and practices.

When we enquired whether they believed in magic or witch craft, only 26.67 per cent of the mother respondents said 'Yes'. In the case of daughter respondents 10 per cent gave an affirmative reply. Scheduled Castes believe in a number of omens. There are good as well as bad omens. A girl carrying a pot of water, vehicles, crying of certain animals and birds etc. are considered as good omen. The approach of a widow, men carrying firewood, cat crossing one's path, etc. are considered as bad omen. The younger generation have no faith in such beliefs.

It was found that cent per cent of the mother respondents had faith in omen. In the case of the daughter respondents, only 36 per cent said that they had belief in it. These changes were mostly due to the impact of education.

Dresses

In the dressing pattern also there was much change. Traditionally, the Scheduled Castes were not allowed to cover the upper part of their body. Today, there are no restrictions for dressing, and they can wear any type of dress they liked. In the case of mother respondents, belonging to Palghat, many did not cover their upper part (a certain age level such as above 50 group) at present also. But their daughters showed a very significant change in mode of dressing.

In earlier times, Scheduled Castes believed that diseases were caused by the dissatisfied spirits and deities. In our study, it was found that if they were taken ill, they all depended on hospitals. Many customs prevailed among Scheduled Castes associated with marriage, child birth, dress and food pattern. But today they are following the customs of higher castes. When we asked whether they followed any customs of higher castes, cent per cent of the mother and daughter respondents said 'Yes'.

Food Habits

In olden days, the Scheduled Castes used utensils made of earthern ware. Now-a days, they are having aluminium and steel utensils for cooking food, just like the higher castes. Another interesting change in food pattern is time of eating. In earlier times, they had only one meal a day. Most often, it was rice porridge and one curry which included tapioca and other roots. But now they are having three meals per day and includes both vegetarian and non-vegetarian items.

Political Participation

Political freedom, just like economic independence, is another important factor, which gives women a better status. The political condition of a nation has its impact on the status of women. There was a time when women were considered unsuitable for any type of political activity and were denied the right to participate in the political process. This was applicable in the case of Scheduled Caste women also.

About two decades ago, the Scheduled Castes had no political powers and had nothing to do with the political powers. After the formation of the Constitution of India, the founding fathers accepted the principle of adult franchise. As a result, Scheduled Castes got the right of voting which elevated their status. "With the introduction of adult franchise and unfettered freedom in political compaigning and participation, the Scheduled Castes gained right to take part in political affairs. Gough also makes a reference to such a situation in Kerala."[16]

"The two important areas of their political participation are in respect of election to village Panchayats and election to the Legislature and Parliament. To the Scheduled Castes who were all along labourers depending entirely on the caste Hindu and other groups of people in the areas, political freedom is a novelty".[17]

We made attempt to find out the extent to which the Scheduled Caste women were interested in politics, or had access to political participation and voting behaviour. Our study showed that the younger generation was active in politics while the older generation was not interested in active politics. The Scheduled Castes in traditional society did not allow women to move about freely in public, so they thought that politics was not a field for women.

While analysing the data regarding membership in political parties it was found that 73.54 per cent of the mother respondents had membership. In the case of daughter respondents, 74.67 per cent of them had the same. They also had participated in strikes, dharnas, ralleys organised by political parties.

16. Kathleen Gough, Palakkara, *Social and Religious Change in Central Kerala*, M.N. Srinivas (ed.), in India's Village, Asia Publishing House, Bombay 1960, pp. 146-147.
17. Mumtaz Ali Khan, *op. cit.*, p. 181.

It was seen that a good number of Scheduled Caste women had active participation in politics. This may be because they were having membership in unions which was affiliated to political parties. Majority of respondents in our study were doing agricultural work and most of the agricultural unions were affiliated to political parties.

65 per cent of the daughter respondents participated frequently in political activities, 20 per cent regularly and only 15 per cent participated rarely. In the case of mother respondents, 58.74 per cent participated frequently, and the remaining rarely. This shows that political participation of Scheduled Caste women of the younger generation increased. The educationwise analysis of mother's data showed that as education increased, the participation also increased.

When asked 'Did you vote in the last election' ? cent per cent of our mother respondents said 'Yes'. In the case of daughter respondents 74.67 per cent of them said 'yes.' The respondents who did not vote gave reasons as they had no vot e or they were being under age for voting.

To the question for "whom did you vote"?, it was found that 62.22 per cent of the mother respondents said that they voted for the candidate which was suggested by their husband, 24.44 per cent voted according to the candidate's political ideology, 10.22 per cent voted because of the candidate's merit and only 3.11 per cent voted because the candidate belonged to the same caste.

It is clear from the table 64 that 44.02 per cent of the younger generation voted because of the candidate's political ideology. At the same time 62.22 per cent of mothers voted for candidates suggested by their husbands. It shows the difference in voting for candidate suggested by others. Younger generation were more educated and they do not want to depend on other's opinions.

TABLE 64

Mothers' and Daughters' Voting Candidate Suggested by Others

Voting for candidate suggested by others	*Mothers'*	*Daughters'*	*Total*
Suggested by the husband	140 63.22%	33 19.64%	173 44.02%
According to candidate's merit	55 24.44%	6 3.57%	61 15.52%
Candidate's political ideology	23 10.22%	68 40.48%	91 23.16%
Candidate belong to same caste	7 3.11%	61 36.31%	68 17.30%
Total	225 100.00%	168 100.00%	393

In the case of daughter respondents, it was found that 40.48 per cent voted on the basis of candidate's political ideology, 36.31 per cent voted on the basis of caste, 19.64 per cent vote d for the candidate suggested by their husbands and 3.57 per cent voted because of candidate's merit. None of them voted on the consideration of candidate's castes. The data was analysed on the basis of education and was found to be related.

It was found that only 7.69 per cent of the illiterate respondents voted voluntarily, 61.54 per cent of the college educated and the majority of the high school and above educated group also voted voluntarily, 26.92 per cent of respondents voted for the candidate suggested by their husbands who belonged to illiterate group. It can be inferred that the more educated respondents had more self reliance on voting behaviour. The educated women did not consult their husbands in this matter. One of the respondents voted on the basis of caste.

70.63 per cent of illiterate respondents voted for the candidate suggested by their husbands. The SSLC and college educated respondents had not consulted their husbands. Among them, 50 per cent voted on the basis of the candidate's merit. The respondents who voted for the candidate of the same caste belonged to illiterate group. Here also education of the respondents was found to have influence. The number of women who voted for candidate of their own choice increased with their education.

Conclusion

This chapter deals with the cultural mobility among Scheduled Caste women of two generations in certain areas such as religion, intercaste relations, social participation, visiting high castes, practice of untouchability, voting behaviour, interdining etc. We also analysed the attitudinal difference regarding age at marriage, preferred age at marriage for girls and boys, attitude towards endogamous marriage, intercast e marriage, cross cousin marriage, arranged marriage, dowry system, joint family system, and family planning.

First we analysed the intercaste relations of Scheduled Castes. It was found that 15 years ago, the majority of mothers never visited higher caste houses. At present 41.33 per cent of daughters visited higher caste's house regularly, but only 4 per cent of mothers did the same. The variables such as age and education were found to have significant relationship with this practice. It was the younger age group and highly educated respondents who visited more than the less educated. Education has contributed a great deal to this change.

It was also found that younger generation had more high-caste friends than elder generation. In both the cases, age, education, occupation and income were the factors contributing to this, of which education had a higher share.

With regard to social partlcipation it was evident that in former days none among the elder generation participated in social functions which high caste people attended. But at present, mother respondents rarely participated in such functions. In the case of daughters, there is some change in this habit. This revealed that social distance was still existing in our society to a certain extent.

All mother respondents considered high caste people's visits to their houses as prestigious. While the younger generation did not consider it so. Age and education were thus the important factors.

It was found that majority of the daughter respondents did not suffer from the practice of untouchability. As against this, the majority of the mothers very often suffered from untouchability. Educationwise analysis showed that in both the generations it was the educated who suffered less from untouchability. So we can infer that education could minimise untouchability.

In the case of interdining also there was considerable difference between the two generations. 51 per cent of the daughters had dined with high castes, while 92 per cent of the mothers said that they never interdined with high castes. Educated respondents were found to interdine more with the high castes.

Another finding was that Scheduled Castes now did not use their caste name with their names. They did not want to reveal their caste identity through names. Education also played an important part in this regard. Educated people never used their caste name.

These findings proved that there is remarkable improvement in intercaste relations and education remain an important factor contributing to this change.

81 per cent of the daughters and 39 per cent of the mothers had membership in caste organistion. Majority of mothers said that due to illiteracy they were unaware of the advantages of caste organisation.

Analysis of data on age at marriage showed that majority of daughters and mothers were married at the age of 15 or below. It was also found that the educated daughter respondents married at the age of 26 and above. This showed that education could influence the age at marriage. In addition to this, the educated respondents tended to suggest higher age at marriage for their children, when compared to the illiterate and the less educated respondents.

Educalion was found to be one of major factors in the formation of attitude of the respondents towards various issues. Majority of the mothers and daughters favoured endogamous marriage, but as the level of education increased, the tendency to insist on endogamous marriage decreased. In the case of intercaste marriage, a small percentage of respondents in both generation approved of the same. The higher the level of education, the lower was the proportion who opposed intercaste marriage. Majority of mothers preferred cross cousin marriage while only 31 per cent of daughters preferred the same Education also had influence in this regard.

Almost all the respondents, in both the generations, were found to be more in favuor of divorce and widow remarriage, and were against payment of dowry.

Majority of the mothers lived in extended families and majority of the daughters lived in nuclear families. Compared to the daughter respondents, the mother respondents had less freedom to express their views in the presence of their husband and also had less role in the decision-making process. With the influence of education and employment opportunities, the younger generation had become more independent and expressive than their mothers.

While analysing, the attitude towards family planning it was found that majority of the mother respondents and cent per cent of the daughter respondents took a favourable attitude. It was found that the educated mothers showed a more favourable attitude. Age and education was found to have considerable influence on the formation of this attitude among our respondents.

There were considerable changes in religious practices and customs between the two generations. Both the mother and the daughter respondents had faith in God. Only a small per cent of mothers had belief in magic and witchcraft. It was found that there was change in the customs regarding marriage, child birth, food pattern and dress. In ancient days, Scheduled Castes followed their own customs related to ceremonies. Today, they began to follow the customs of higher castes more or less in the same manner.

Our data showed that both the mothers and the daughters had membership in political parties. There was only a slight difference in membership between two generations. In the case of participation, the younger generation were active. Votihg behaviour also showed the same trend.

These findings supported our fifth hyopothesis that there is greater mobility in the attitudes and reactions of Scheduled Caste women towards many common social issues and education is the major contributing factor.

CHAPTER VI

Case Study

Data analysis in chapters III, IV and V clearly indicated social mobility among Scheduled Caste women, in several areas, such as education; occupation, social status and intercaste relations. With the intention of acquiring in-depth knowledge into the various aspects of the problem, two typical cases (of three generations) were selected from Kariyam ann Venganoor, in Trivandrum district. These case studies support the major findings of the empirical study.

Selection of cases faced many problems. It was difficult to identify cases which has mobility within the three generations. When such cases were located, the respondents were not co-operative in providing information. They feared that their life histories will be published which would reveal their identity. Since the respondents would be away for work or engaged in household work, several visits were required to collect information from the three generations. Occasional visits were very helpful for understanding changes in the family structure and function. The data was collected through careful observation, interview schedule, and free flowing intervies and discussions.

CASE A

Mala is a 76 year old Scheduled Caste (pulaya) woman who lives in Sreekaryam Panchayat of Trivadrum district. She is a widow having seven children. Two of her children are working in the State Government service and other work as coolies. Her husband was an agriculture labourer. Her income per month is Rs. 40/-.

Mala is an illiterate agriculture workers. She told that lack of encouragement from her parents and financial problems were the main reasons for her illiteracy. Moreover, she had to help her parents who were also agriculture labourers. Instead of wages, she got food from the land owner. During her childhood she was not aware of any of the educational facilities provided to Scheduled Castes by the Government, but at present, she is aware about them. She wanted to learn to read and write, but could not get opportunity to attend school. She also remembered that in those days, Scheduled Castes were not permitted to attend schools. Even though she is illiterate, she wanted her children, especially the boys, to be well educated. However, because of repeated failures, five of her children had to discontinue their studies prematurely. The other two had passed SSLC examination and some technical courses and have got modern jobs.

In Mala's opinion, both the aim and advantage of education is improvement of one's status in society. She strongly believed that education is instrumental for individuals socal status. She was of the opinion that women's education is necessary, but not a must for securing a good job. Though she considered education as a status—raising factor, it is not fetching acceptance from other castes. In her view, high caste people will never consider Scheduled Castes as equals, even if the latter were educated. Mala had respect towards educated people in her community.

Mala had not visited the houses of high caste people regularly or frequently, before fifteen years and even at present, she rarely visits such houses. She had no high caste friends. She recalled that in early days, she was not allowed to enter their houses. Mala was aware that the intensity of 'social distance' has decreased to some extent, but for a person of her sort, making company with high castes is unimaginable even now. She never participated in social functions, which the high caste people attended. Neither she was invited to dine with the latter nor she had friends among them. The high castes never took even drinking water from their house. Mala referred to high caste people as "Thampurakkal" and people of her own caste as "Malappulayai" and felt that the Thampurakkal visiting a Malappulayai's house is something honourable and prestigious.

Mala has been engaged in agriculture work for the fifty five years. Infact, her parents and other family members were also doing agriculture work. She admitted her preference to do traditional work, because she thought that, this is what is meant for them. She also believed that modern occupation is not meant for them. Mala was sad, she said that ancient society denied them education and modern jobs. Mala expected better occupational prospects for her educated children. But she is satisfied with her present job, income, and status. According to her, as a Scheduled Caste, she has to be satisfied with her present job, income and status. She recalled that in earlier days, the condition of Scheduled Castes was much worse than at present.

Analysing the causes for the low status of Scheduled Castes in society, Mala pointed out that the major reason for this situation is not only the traditional occupation, but also the lower caste membership the individuals hold is partly contributing to the situation. She also believed that improvement in occupational pattern would not help to release them from subservience to the higher castes. She felt that the Scheduled Castes can never enjoy a status equal to that of high castes, even if they reach the same occupation as the high castes do. She was of the opinion that if she belonged to a high caste, she would have had better chances for social advancement. Mala sufferred from untouchability to a great extent.

Mala got married at the age of eleven. Commenting on the age at marriage, she said that she preferred 18 years for girls and 20 for boys. Her attitude towards endogamy is favourable because the in-laws had special concern for the married couples in such cases and the treatment will be different from that of their counterparts in other cases. Mala's attitude towards inter-caste marriage is unfavourable. She did not think that Scheduled Castes can improve their caste status by intercaste marriage. Her attitude towards cross-cousin marriage is also unfavourable. She was of the opinion that cross-cousin marriage contributes to strong and healthy familial relations. In the case of children's marriage, sho would like to approve arranged marriage. According to Mala, dowery is undesirable and she did not pay any dowery at the time of her marriage.

Mala lived with her son and her family is an exended family. According to Mala, joint family system is good and its advantages are many such as social security of old age people, co-operative in the family etc.

While discussing about decision-making on family matters, Mala said that she never got a chance to express her views regarding the family matters. After her husband's death, her son is the head of the family.

Mala had favourable attitud towards family planning, though she did not practice it and opined that a couple should have less than five children. She preferred boys to girls, for she believed that female children will be a liability to their parents.

Coming to the religious practices, Mala said that she is worshipping the diety "Marutha" in our house, and she also visits temple, occasionally. She always prayed to Kuladevathas. Besides, she believed in spirits, witchcraft and magic and thought that dissatisfaction of Kuldevathas caused many diseases to the family members. She had belief in omen, for example, crossing by a cat, chattering of certain birds etc. are considered as bad omen.

Recalling the marriage customs, Mala said that in ancient society, Scheduled Castes did not have many customs, other than *thalikettu* and giving *kachchamuri.* Wearing gold ornaments was not common. On the marriage day, the bridegrooms sister, standing behind the bride, would tighten the knot of a black thread having the '*Thali*'. Bridegroom gives a now white cloth called *Kachachamvri* and with this, the marriage ceremony is completed. She said that the dressing pattern among Scheduled Castes has also changed a lot. Her mother and grand mother did not use blouses.

During the earlier period, their food habits were different. They had only one meal a day i.e., in the evening. They used vessels made of clay and earthen pot for cooking. She never went for cinema and had no other entertainments.

Mala is still not a member of any caste organisation and is unware of such organisations and their functions.

She had membership in a political party, but had never participated in their activities. She was compelled to take membership of the party for getting agriculture pension. She did vote in the last election to the candidate suggested by her son.

Mala had 4 cents of land in her name. She divided her land

among her children. She gave more property to girls than boys. She had no savings.

Mala thought that in these days, when compared to the earlier times, the status of Scheduled Castes have improved.

Kalu

Kalu, daughter of Mala is 52 year old and is the headmistress of a Government Lower Primary School. She had an intercaste marriage and her husband belongs to a high caste. He is an ex-service man. She had an income of Rs. 1000/- per month. She had four daughters and three of them are married. None of them had jobs. The youngest daughter is a post-graduate student in homeo medicine.

Kalu had passed SSLC and TTC. She was self motivated for higher studies. She was aware of the welfare measures through media like radio, newspaper etc., and had utilized the facilities partially. Kalu wanted to study up to graduation but could not. Now she wished that her children (both boys and girls) could be educated to any extent they aspired for. She proudly said that none of her children stopped their studies prematurely. Three of them had successfully completed graduation and the fourth one is still engaged in studies.

In Kalu's view, the aim of education is for getting a modern job. She is convinced that the main advantage of education is for improving status and believed that education is a status indicator especially for Scheduled Castes. She strongly agreed that women's education is a must in our society. As against her mother, Kalu stressed the point that education will definitely fetch acceptance from other castes. She thought that, most often, in an ordinary social interaction, an educated member of Scheduled Caste will be treated as equal to a high caste member of the same educational qualification. She agreed that to some extent, high caste people will consider Scheduled Castes as equals, if they are educated. Kalu had no special respect towards educated people in her community. She considered them as equals.

Kalu had rarely visited the houses of high caste people before fifteen years, but at present, she visits them frequently and also had a good number of friends among them. She recalled that in former days she never participated in social functions which high caste people attended, but these days, she very often participates in such fuctions. In the same manner, in their family, they had high caste guests. She told that sometimes high castes take food from Scheduled Caste's house. She was also invited to dine with them when she visited high castes. She never used her caste name with her name. She did not feel high caste people's visit to their house as prestigious.

As against her mother's occupation, Kalu had a modern job viz., teacher. She left the traditional occupation because of its casual nature and low wages. She had 28 years of service in the present job. She had no previous employment ; and had never gone for traditional jobs. She is satisfied with her present occupation, income and status. She got the job with the help of the reservation policy of the Government. In her opinion job, education, style of life, wealth and behaviour were the factors which bring status to low castes. She also added that the benefit of modern occupation is high status, high income, and opportunities for more social contacts which may decrease social disabilities.

While discussing about the causes for the low status of Scheduled Castes in society, Kalu considered low standard of of living as the major reason. She argued that improvement in accupational pattern would help them to release from subservience to the high castes. She felt that the Scheduled Castes can, to a certain extent, enjoy a status equal to that of high castes, only if they reach the same occupation as the high castes do. Kalu did not think that if she belonged to a high caste, she would have better chance for socal advancement. She never suffered from untouchability.

Kalu got married at the age of twenty-one. Discussion on the age of marriage, she said that the preferred above 25 years for girls and above 30 years for boys. She preferred her own children to marry after attaining better livelihood. Though she is favourable to endogamy, she was not insisting on it in the case of her children. She was against cross-cousin marriage but not against intercaste marriage. She thought that to a certain extent, Scheduled Castes can improve caste status by intercaste marriage. Her marriage was an intercaste one. She believed that cross-cousin marriage will cause many problems such as conflict among family members, and hereditary diseases etc. Kalu would like to arrange her children's marriage with the consent of them. She also had unfavourable attitude towards dowery.

Kalu and nuclear family. Three of her daughters were married and they lived separately. According to Kalu, joint family system had many disadvantages like problems due to generation gap, communication gap, economic handicap etc.

While talking about decision-making in family matters, Kalu said that she and her husband jointly take such decisions.

Kalu had favourable attitude towards family planning and had also practiced it. In her opinion, a couple should have 2 to 3 children. She had no special preference to male child. Kalu had four daughters and she added that she could not find any problems with female children.

Regarding practices of religious beliefs and customs, she is following the customs of high caste. Her family had no separate diety for worshipping. Kalu also used to visit temples.

Recalling the marriage customs, she told that she is following high caste's customs Discussing about dressing pattern, she found so much change among Scheduled Castes.

Kalu used vessls made of aluminium and earthen pots for cooking. Food habit is not different from high castes. Occasionally, she went for recreational activities.

Though Kalu is aware of caste organisation, she is not a member of that organisation.

Kalu had no membership in any political party, she did vote in the last election to the candidate of her own choice.

She had 50 cents of land and is readi to give equal share for all children.

Sathi

Sathi, the grand daughter of Mala and the daughter of Kalu, is 24 years old. She is a postgraduate student in homeo medicine. She is unmarried and had no self income. Her parents were having modern occupation.

Compared to her grand mother, Sathi is highly educated. Sathi was motivated by her parents for higher studies. She was aware of the educational facilities provided to Scheduled Castes by the Government, through radio, newspaper etc. Sathi expected that her children would be educated to a higher level.

In her view, the aim of education if for getting a job other than traditional. She pointed out that the advantage of education is that it helps to improve one's status. She strongly agreed that education is a vehicle for status improvement. In her opinion, women's education is a must in our society. Sathi supported the fact that education is highly important for status improvement and it also improves living conditions of Scheduled Castes. She also believed that, to some extent, education fetch them acceptance from other castes. Sathi behaves as equals towards the educated Scheduled Castes.

Sathi visited the houses of high caste people frequently and also had a number of friends among them. In her house she had higher caste guests for social fuctions and interdining is very common on such occasions. She did not feel such visits as prestigious.

Analysing the causes for the low status of Scheduled Castes in society, Sathi pointed out that the major reason is traditional occupation and low caste membership. She told that job, education, wealth, style of life and behaviour were the factors which bring status to Scheduled Castes. She argued that by getting modern occupations one can get high status, high income, and chances for more social contacts and this will decrease social disabilities. She was of the opinion that in an ordinary social interaction, most often, an educated member of Scheduled Caste will be treated as an equal to high caste member of same educational qualification. Sathi did not think that if she belonged to a high caste, she would have had better chance for social advancement. She never had suffered from untouchability.

Commenting on the age at marriage, she said that she preferred the girls to marry at the age of 28 and the boys to marry at 30 years. She is not assisting on endogamy, but had a favourable attitude. Sathi's attitude towards intercaste marriage and cross-cousin marriage is unfavourable. She also pointed out the bad effects of cross-cousin marriage. According to Sathi, dowry is undesirable.

Sathilives in a nuclear family and is against joint family. According to her, joint family had more disadvantages than advantages. In a joint family system, conflict is natural. Economic burden for head of the family is another enven in joint family.

Sathi had favourable attitude towards family planning. She opined that a couple should have one or two children either boys and girls. She had no special preference for boys or girls.

Sathi said that they are following the religious practices and customs of high castes. She had no separate deity for worshipping. She goes to temple occasionally. She had belief in God, but not in spirits, witchcrafts, magic or omen. She, like her mother, also take allopathic treatment during illness.

They used three meals per day. The vessels were made of aluminium and steel.

Though Sathi is aware of caste organisation and its functions, she is not a member in any of them.

She had no membership in any political party and never had participated in political activities.

Sathi had no property of her own. She had the habit of reading newspaper, magazine, weekly etc.

From the three generations of Scheduled Caste women viz. grand mother, mother and daughter, we found mobility in many areas. There is considerable educational mobility among these generations. Whereas, Mala, the grand mother is illiterate, her daughter is educated upto SSLC and TTC, and Sathi the grand daughter, is a post-graduate student. There is also mobility in the level of enucational aspirations and awareness about various welfare programmes implemented by the government.

The level of educational aspiration of the second and the third generations is very high, when compared to first generation. In the case of awareness and utilisation of welfare measure the same trend is seen.

The trend in occupational mobility shows that there is inter-generational vertical occupational mobility. While grand mother is engaged in agriculture work, their traditional occupation, her daughter is working as headmistress in LP school; and her grand daughter (after completion of her course) will be a homeo doctor. We also found mobility in preference of occupation, attitude towards children's occupation, stisfactson with social status etc. The second and third generations preferred to do modern jobs while the first generation preferred to continue their traditional occupation.

There are changes in areas such as igter-caste relations, social participation, practice of untouchability, membership in caste organisation, age at mariage, and attitudinal difference on various social issues like cross-cousin marriage, inter-caste marriage, endogamous marriage, attitude towards family planning and practice of family planning. In all matters such as higher caste visits, having higher caste friends, interdining, and social participation, there is much difference between the three generations.

CASE B

Neeli

Neeli is an 88 year old Pulaya woman who lives at Vanganoor, in Trivandrum district. She is a widow having eight children. None of her children are having modern occupation. Her husband was an agriculture labourer. Her monthly income is Rs. 50.

Neeli is illiterate and the reason for her illiteracy was financial problem. She wanted to learn to read and write but also thought that education is not necessary for women. When her parents went for work, she had to remain at home rearing the young ones. Neeli told that during her childhood she was not aware of the welfare measures provided to Scheduled Castes by the government, but, at present she is aware of some such facilities. She wanted her children to be educated upto SSLC. She sadly complained that none of her children passed even the

4th standard. Because of repeated failures, her children had to stop studies prematurely.

In Neeli's opinion, the aim of education is for improving status in society. Neeli argued that education is a good medium for gaining social status. Inspite of this, she was of the opinion that women's education is not neeessary. She considered education as a status raising factor, but it is not fetching acceptance from high castes. She commented that high caste people will never consider Scheduled Castes as equals. even if the latter were educated. Neeli had respect towards educated people in her community.

Neeli had not visited the houses of higher caste people in the past or at present. She had no high caste friends, and in her opinion for a pesson of her sort making company with high castes is not imaginable even now. Neeli never participated in social functions which the high caste people attended. She was never invited to dine with high castes. The high castes never took even drinking water from their house. She considered high caste people's visit to Scheduled Caste's house as prestigious.

Neeli is doing agriculture work for the last 70 years. Her parents and other family members were also engaged in the same work. She preferred to do traditional occupation because she thought that as low caste, she deserved only lower jobs such as scavenging, sweeping, etc. Neeli believed that modern occupation is not meant for them. She is satisfied with her present job, income, and status. According to her as a Scheduled Caste, she has to be satisfied with her present position. She recalled that in earlier days, the condition of Scheduled Castes was much worse than today.

Analysing the causes for the low status of Scheduled Castes society, Neeli pointed out that lower standard of living and traditional occupation are the main reasons. But she believed that occupational improvement would not help them to release from subservience to the higher castes. She felt that the Scheduled Castes can never enjoy a status equal of high castes, even if they do the same occupation as the high castes do. She was of the opinion that, if she belonged to a high caste, she would have had better chance for social advancement. Neeli had suffered from untouchability to a great extent.

Neeli was married at the age of twelve. Discussing about the age at marriage she said that she preferred 16 years for girls and 20 for boys. Her attitude towards endogamy is favourable. She told that the family relations will be strengthened by cross cousin marriage. She is against intercaste maıriage and thought that Scheduled Castes cannot improve their caste status through intercaste marriage. In the case of children's marriage, she would like to have arranged marriage. According to Neeli, dowry is undesirable and she did not pay any dowary at the time of her marriage.

Neeli lived with her daughter and her family is an extended one. According to Neeli, Joint family system is good and the advantages are many; such as social security to old age people, co-operation in the family, special concern for elder members in the family etc.

Commenting about decision-making in family matters, Neeli complained that she never got a chance to express he views regarding the family matters.

Neeli had favourable attitude towards family planning, though she did not practice it and opined that a couple should have five to six children. She had no preference to male children.

Neeli is worshipping separate God 'Thampuran' in her house; and rarely she goes to temple. She believes in spirits, witchcraft and magic and also thought that dissatisfaction of 'Thampuran' and other Kuladevathas causes many diseases to the family members. She never went to hospital for treatment of illness but used only indigenous medicines. Most often she tried to propitiate 'kuladevathas.

Recalling the marriage customs, Neeli said that in ancient society, they did not have many customs, other than '*taliketti*' and giving '*Kachchamuri*'. It was so amazing her that today their people were also wearing fashionable dresses. In the case of dressing pattern she told that there is so much change. She did not wear blouse at present, as well as in the past.

Their food habits during ancient days were entirely different from today's. Most often, they had only one meal a day. They used only vessels made of clay. But today they had three meals per day and used vessels made of steel and aluminium. She did not have the habit of going for entertainments. Though Neeli is a member of caste organisation, she has not participated in their activities.

Neeli took membership of a political party for getting agricultural pension. She was compelled to take membership by local political workers. She had participated in their activities such as pensioners' strike etc. She voted in the last election for the candidate which was suggested by her son.

Neeli had no property and savings of her own. She agreed that in these days, when compared to their earlier times, the status of Scheduled Castes have improved.

Chinna

Chinna, daughter of Neeli is 62 years old. She and her husband are agricultural labourers. She had an income of Rs. 100 per month. Chinna had five children, all of them married. Two of her daughters are in modern jobs.

Chinna had studied upto the 4th standard. Because of family responsibility, she could not continue her studies. She was not aware of educational facilities provided to Scheduled Castes by the government at that time, but now she is aware of these. She got information from radio, newspaper and also from other Scheduled Caste members. She wanted to study upto high school level. In the case of her children's education, she desired them to be educated to any extent they wanted, two of her children discontinued studies because of repeated failures.

In Chinna's opinion the aim of education is for getting a government job. She considered the advantage of education as improvement in status. She agreed that women's education is a must in our society. Chinna also had the opinion that education is a status raising factor and one can improve his/her living condition, by education. She also thought that educated people will get more acceptance from members of other castes. Chinna considered that education fetches social acceptance from high castes and agreed that, to some extent, high caste people will consider Scheduled Castes as equals if they are educated. Chinna had respect towards educated people in her community.

Chinna had never visited high caste's house before fifteen years, but at present she visits frequently. In early days, she never participated in social functions which high caste people attended, but these days she participates in such functions though rarely. In the same manner, in Scheduled Caste's social functions, they had high caste friends. Chinna was never invited to dine with high castes when she visited their houses. She considered high caste people's visit to their house as prestigious.

Chinna is doing agriculture work for the last fifty years. She prefers to do modern occupation, but is also aware that there is no chance for getting government job since she is not having enough education. She expected better occupational prospects for her educated children. She is satisfied with her present job, income, and status.

Analysing the causes for the low status of Scheduled Castes in society, Chinna considered traditional occupation, and low standard of living as the major reasons. She also believed that Scheduled Castes will not get any status equal to high castes even if they reach the same occupation as the higher castes do. She was of the opinion that if she belonged to a high caste, she would have better chances for social advancement. Chinna suffered from untouchability to a great extent.

Chinna got married at the age of sixteen. She said that she preferred 20 years for girl and above 25 years for boys. She insisted on endogamous marriage and had unfavourable attitude towards intercaste marriage. She did not think that Scheduled Castes can improve their caste status through intercaste marriage. She likes crosscousin marriage. Chinna would like to arrange her children's marriage with the consent of parents. She had unfavourable attitude towards dowry. However, she had given dowry for her daughter's marriage.

Chinna lived with her daughter. Chinna had pointed out more advantages of joint family than disadvantages.

While talking about decision-making in the family, Chinna said that she and her husband always jointly take decisions in the family.

Chinna had favourable attitude towards family planning, though she did not practice it, and opined that a couple should have less than five children. She had no special preference to male child.

Coming to religious practices, Chinna told that she is not worshipping separate deities. She had belief in Kuladevathas. To a certain extent, she believed in spirits; magic and witchcraft. Occasionally, she visits temples. For curing diseases, she depends on allopathic hospitals.

Recalling the marriage customs, Chinna said that in early days, Scheduled Castes had no special customs. Today, they are followed the customs of high castes. She said that the dressing pattern among Scheduled Castes has also changed a lot. Her mother and grand mother did not wear blouses.

In the case of food habits, it was different in early days. Most often, they had only one meal a day. In olden days, they used only vessels made of earthenware. Now-a-days, they are having steel, and aluminium vessels.

Chinna had membership in caste organisation but never participated in their activities.

She was compelled to take membership in political party for getting agriculture pension. She did vote in the last election according to the candidate's merit.

Chinna had 16 cents of land and her hohse has tiled roof. She had no savings.

In her opinion, the conditions of Scheduled Castes have improved a great deal compared to early days.

Vasantha

Vasantha, the grand daughter of of Neeli and daughter of Chinna, is 30 years old. She is working as a typist in a government office. Her husband is also working as a clerk in the same office. He is a high caste man. She had an income of Rs. 1,500 per month. She had two children both of them studying in English medium schools.

Vasantha had passed pre-degree and type writing, she told that she was self motivated for her higher studies. During her student life, she was aware of the educational facilities provided to Scheduled Castes by the government through the teachers. In her school, one of the high caste teacher was very helpful by providing these information. The teacher also encouraged her in her studies. Though she aspired for graduation, she could not achieve it due to financial problems. She expected her children would be educated to any extent they desired.

According to Vasantha, education helps to achieve modern job. Vasantha agreed that women's education is a must in our society. Especially in the case of Scheduled Caste women, education is inevitable for their development. In her opinion education is a must for securing a job and for improving social status. She believed that to a certain extent education can fetch them acceptance from members of other castes. Vasantha had no special respect towards educated people in her community and considered them as equals.

Occasionally, Vasantha visited high caste's house. She is proud of the fact that she got change in her childhood for visiting high castes. Now she had a number of high caste friends. Very often she participated in social functions which also attended by high caste people. She also used to invite high caste friends for social functions in her house and is being invited by them. She was also invited to dine with high castes. She never used her caste name with her name. She did not feel high caste's visit to her house as prestigious.

Because of the low income and low status she had left traditional work and joined government service. When she was a student, she used to go for traditional work with her mother. After getting the present job, she never went for such work. She is now satisfied with her present job, status and income. She got the job with the help of the reservation provided to Scheduled Castes by the government.

In her opinion, education, way of living, and wealth, were the factors which bring status to Scheduled Castes. She considered the benefit of modern occupation as high status, high income and chance for social contacts with high castes. She added that modern occupation decreases social discriminiation.

While discussing about the causes for the low status of Scheduled Castes in society, Vasantha considered low standard of living as the major one. She believed that caste as such had no significance today. If a man is wealthy, he will have status in society. From her own experience, she proclaimed that most often in an ordinary social interaction an educated member of Scheduled Castes will be treated as equal to a high caste member of same educational qualification.

Vasantha got married at the age of 23. She is of the opinion that giris should be married at the age of above 26 and boys at 30 years. She thought that to a certain extent, Scheduled Castes can improve their caste status by intercaste marriage. Vasantha pointed out the disadvantages of cross cousin marriage; and is against dowry system.

Vasantha's family is nuclear type. In her view, joint family creates many problems.

While discussing about decision-making in the family, Vasantha said that most often she and her husband jointly take decisions. Rarely her husband alone will take certain decisions.

She had favourable attitude towards family planning and is also practicing it. In her view, a couple should have on or two children. She had no preference for boys or girls.

In the case of religious beliefs and customs, she is following the customs of high castes. In her house, there is no separate deity for worshipping and had no belief in magic or witchcraft. She never depended on such practices for curing diseases. Occasionally she visits temple.

Regarding the marriage customs, she told that she is following high caste customs. She said that there is so much change in the pattern of dressing today, when compared to earlier days.

In her house, she used steel and aluminium vessels for cooking, and other purposes. When compared to early times, the are having three to four times meals per day.

Neither she is a member of caste organisation, nor a political party. She had her own political ideas and voted in the last election according to political ideal.

Vasantha had 18 cents of land as her own. She lives in a terraced house. She had savings in bank.

In these three cases, we found mobility in education, occupation and cultural spheres. There is considerable change in educatiohal level from grand mother to grand daughter. There is educational mobility within the three generations. Neeli the grand mother is an illiterate, Chinna her daughter is primary level educated, and Vasantha had college level education. Here we found slight educational mobility among the first and second generation. In the case of the third generation, there is greater educational mobility from first generation. The low level of aspiration and lack of awareness about educational facilities provided to Scheduled Castes were the factors contributing to the difference of first generation with second and third generations.

In the case of occupational mobility, there is no inter-generational mobility between the first and the second generations. However, in the case of third generation, there is vertical occupational mobility. While the grand mother and her daughter were agriculture labourers, her grand daughter was doing modern job (working as a typist in government service).

There is also difference in opinion on preference to occupation, attitude towards children's occupation, satisfaction with present job, and social status.

In the case of the first two generations, there is not much change i.e., both of them were traditional workers and their view point regarding many issues were more or less similar. In the case of third generation there was change in areas such as intercaste relations, social participation, practice of untouchability membership in caste organisation, age at marriage and attitudinal difference in various social issues like cross cousin, marriage, intercaste marriage, endogamous marriage and family planning. In almost all matters, the first generation and the second generation had shared more or less the same view, while the view of the third generation is significantly different from that of the other two generations. There is change even in the case of name.

In this case, education, modern occupation, flexible inter-caste relations, change in the attitudes etc., were found to be the important factors contributing to social mobility among Scheduled Caste women.

CHAPTER VII

Summary of Findings

The objective of the present study was to find out whether there is social mobility among the Scheduled Caste women in Kerala, and if so, to identify the factors responsible for it. It was also intended to assess the areas where mobility is clearly pronounced. And finally, if there is no mobility, to find out the factors responsible for it. Accordingly, we formulated the following hypotheses :

Hypotheses

Our central hypotheses is that there is social mobility among Scheduled Caste women, and education had contributed to the same. The sub-hyotheses are :

1. There is considerable educational mobility within the two generations of Scheduled Caste women.
2. Inter-generational occupational mobility is vertical among Scheduled Caste women, though intragenerational occupational mobility is horizontal.

3. Inferiority feelings, prevalent among the Scheduled Caste women, prevent their educational attainment and consequently contributes to their low rate of occupational mobility.

4. Occupational improvement contributes to the social status of Scheduled Caste women.

5. There is greater mobility in the attitudes and reactions of Scheduled Caste women towards many common social issues.

A sample of 450 Scheduled Caste women of two generations were chosen for the study. Of the 450 women, 225 were mothers and 225 were their daughters. On the basis of the rate of Scheduled Caste population, three districts, viz. Palghat, Alleppey and Trivandrum were selected for drawing sample. The sample was selected by using stratified random sampling method. With the help of carefully designed two separate interview schedules, we interviewed these 450 Scheduled Caste women.

Analysis of our data (3rd chapter) prove the first hypothesis that there is considerable educational mobility between the two generations of Scheduled Caste women. In every institutional sphere, education has contributed to the social mobility. It is clear that a great majority of daughter respondents were literate, while a large number of mother respondents were illiterate. Thus, the daughter respondents had a level of education higher than their mothers. The level of education of education of our respondents were influenced by variables like age, caste, place of birth, and income. The younger generation was better educated than the elder generation. It may be noted that the youngr age groups were provided with educational facilities, opportunities and welfare measures by the Government. Though Scheduled Castes in general are educationally backward, there was variation in the level of education among the different caste groups within them. Thandans and Sambavas had relatively higher education. In these two caste groups, the children did not have to help their parents in traditional work. In the case of other Scheduled Castes, the children had to help their parents in traditional work such as agriculture, transplanting, weeding etc. Thus higher education come to be plausible for them. District-wise analysis also showed significant influence on the level of education of our respondents. Educationally forward areas had the most educated people. Parent's economic status was also found to be an important factor influencing education.

The uneducated mother respondents expressed the following reasons, in the order of priority for their illiteracy: financial problems, the belief that women's education is unnecessary, lack of pressure from the parents, family responsibility, great distance between home and school, and illtreatment from high caste teachers. The illiterate daughter respondents gave the reasons slightly different from that of their mothers. The reasons given by them were : lack of pressure from parents, belief that women's education is unnecessary, family responsibility, and economic handicap of parents. The main difference between the two generations was that the daughters did not have the problem of schools being far off, nor had they suffered from illtreatment from high caste teachers. Today, untouchability is not a common practice and nobody dares to hurt Scheduled Castes for fear or legal punishment. Another difference was that, when financial problem was an important reason for the illiteracy of mothers, it was not so in the case of their daughters. Today, the Government has implemented many measures, enhancing the educational facilities for Scheduled Castes, which lessen the intensity of their economic hardship. As compared to elder generation, the younger generation is able to utilize more facilities. Another point in favour of the younger generation was that, they had educated mothers who took interest in their education.

Education of the mother respondents seemed to be significantly influencing the educational level of the daughter respondents i.e., higher the education of the mothers, the higher was the educational level of their daughters. The phenomenon of highly educated mothers having illiterate daughters was totally absent. It was found that the educated parents were in a better position to provide their children with proper guidance and motivation for higher education.

Another point that emerged from the study was that the majority of mother respondents were unaware of the educational facilities provided to Scheduled Castes by the government and those who were aware of these facilities had made their full utilization.

There was also difference in the level of educational aspiration between the two generations. The younger generation was highly ambitious than the elder generation. The younger generation was more aware of the value and advantages of education. The daughter respondents considered education as a must for women, while only a small percentage of the mothers thought so. About 50 per cent of the mothers stated that their objective in getting education was for status improvement. On the other hand, a significant majority of daughter respondents aimed at getting better job. While the elder generation believed that education could redeem their status, the younger generation gave importance to modern occupation which would improve their economic status. This was made clear when they were asked about the benefit of education. For the daughters, the benefit of education was that it would help them to get modern jobs. But for the mothers it was a means for status improvement.

Another area where we found difference between the two generations was the education of their children. The elder generation wanted to educate only their sons to the maximum extent possible. But the daughters respondents, opined that they wanted equal education for boys and girls.

In contrast to their mothers, cent per cent of the daughters said that education could improve their living conditions. Besides, they considered that education brought them acceptance from other castes.

Regarding the community's reaction to its educated members, it was found that the majority of the mothers said they showed much respect. The disparity between educated and uneducated was less within the younger generation, but there was much difference between the two generations.

The occupational mobility between the two generations of women showed inter generational vertical trend. About 70 per cent of the mothers were engaged in traditional work, whereas only 30 per cent of their daughters were doing the same occupation and only about 8 per cent of the remaining were in modern occupation. To some extent, we can consider this as intergenerational vertical occupational mobility. Since the mothers were either agricultural workers or other labourers and had no change in their status and remuneration of work, they showed an intra-generational horizontal occupational mobiliy. In the case of daughter respondents, we found that, those who were engaged in modern jobs had change in remuneration, functions of work and social status. So, their intra-generational occupational mobility showed a vertical trend. These findings help us to prove our second hypothesis that, the inter-genera tional occupational mobility, was vertical thoughtless and intra generational mobility was horizontal.

Higher education is the only solution which will make the Scheduled Castes fit for modern occupation. Even for reservation of seats in government jobs minimum educational qualification is essential. When compared to mothers, the number of literate daughters were more and we could see that there was educational mobility among the two generations. However, among the literates, only 5 per cent were educated upto pre-degree while 7 per cent were graduates. The low rate of highly educated Scheduled Caste women may be due to certain particular reasons pertaining to them. If a student fails in one class, he or she is eligible for only fifty per cent of the lumpsum grant from the government. The parents do not seem to bother about their children's further studies without full financial assistance from the government. Another reason is that they do not consider it necessary for women to be educated, hence they do not persuade their daughters for higher education. A third reason is that, since many of the Scheduled Caste women work outside their home to earn a living, the responsibility of home-management and nurturing the younger ones will be on these grown up daughters. Thus, very often, they are forced to discontinue their studies, and are denied the opportunities for higher education. Another fact that hinders their educational mobility was the strong belief prevailing among the Scheduled Caste women that neither education or employment will improve their caste status. Thus, owing to all the reasons cited above, Scheduled Caste were not able to avail themselves of the opportunities for higher education and there by are denied the opportunities for modern occupation.

The economic position of the respondents of the two generations was almost similar, except in the case of daughters having modern occupation. Of the two generations, the younger age groups preferred to do modern occupation. We have proved this by analysing their income, education, and place of birth. The majority of mothers and daughters, who are engaged in traditional jobs, were not satisfied with their jobs, because of the casual nature and low wages.

The state government is providing the Scheduled Castes with training-cum-production centres, which train them in crafts, basket weaving, tailaring etc., which only the daughters' generation had the opportunities to avail. But one main point to be noted is that, the training which is in traditional jobs did not help them to get modern jobs.

Another fact which emerged from our study was participation of women in trade union activities. The majority of mother respondents and cent per cent of the daughter respondents had membership in unions, though there was variation in participation between the two groups.

The majority of the elder generation, and less than 50 per cent of the younger generation, considered that occupational improvement would not help them to be relieved from subservience to the higher castes. They had a strong belief that, being a subordinate caste, they deserved only a low status. This belief was inculcated in them through the socialization process, which resulted in building up an inferiority complex particularly among the lower income group, less educated, and elder age groups and in having little hope in the occupational improvement. These complexes might prevent them from aspiring to acquire modern occupation. These findings prove our third hypothesis that inferiority feelings still prevail among the Scheduled Caste women, which prevent their educational attainment and consequently contribute to their low rate of occupational mobility.

The study also revealed that there is difference in the attitude and opinion among respondents in traditional work and in modern jobs. The mothers in modern jobs had daughters in modern occupation. As against the traditional workers, the respondents in modern occupation were satisfied with their income and occupation. In the case of their status in society, both the generations were dissatisfied. The respondents in modern jobs also stressed that modern occupation helped them to get more social contacts, which in turn, had decreased social disabilities.

Studying the social status of respondents in modern occupation, it was found that they had more freedom of movement, enjoyed a better role in decision-making process, had freedom to spend their money and had membership and participation in cultural activities. Their attitudinal difference was also remarkable. The respondents in modern occupation, preferred higher age at marriage for boys and girls. They opined that children's marriage should be settled by the parents only after consultation with the children. There was also attitudinal difference towards certain common issues such as dowry, endogamous marriage, divorce, family planning, equality for men and women etc. It is significant to note that they advocated intercaste marriage and were against dowry and cross-cousin marriage. These findings helped us to prove the fourth hypothesis that occupational improvement contributed to the social status of Scheduled Caste women.

Another significant finding was that the higher age group, the lower income group, and illiterates wanted their children to stick on to their traditionhl work, while the respondents in modern occupation, the younger age group, and the educated, wanted to keep their children away from caste occupation.

It was noted that a majority of mothers, fifteen years ago, never visited the houses of the high castes. Even now the position has not changed much in their case. In contrast to this, about 50 per cent of the daughter respondents visited the houses of the high castes regutarly. Education has contributed a great deal to this variation and subsequently in acquiring high caste friends. The older generation, who were illiterates or less educated, had no high caste friends.

In early days, Scheduled Castes were not allowed to participate in social functions which the high caste people attended. Even at present the elder generation rarely participated in such functions. In the case of daughters this trend changed and they attended social function where high caste were also present. The analysis revealed that education played an important role in reducing the social distance between the high castes and low castes.

It was also seen that, all the mother respondents had considered visits from the higher caste people to their houses to be prestigious, while none of the daughter respondents throught so. Generational differences and education were the factors which were responsible for this variation.

Regarding practice of untouchability, whereas an overwhelmingly large number of mother respondents very often suffered from untouchability, majority of the daughter respondents did not face such problems. In both the cases, it was the educated group, who suffered less from untouchability. So we can infer that education is a powerful instrument in minimising untouchability.

There was also variation among the Scheduled Caste women of the two generations with regard do interdining. More than 50 per cent of the daughters had dined with high castes, while almost all the mothers said that they never interdined with the high castes. It was found that the educated respondents interdined more frequently with the higher castes.

Another fact revealed from the study was that none of our respondents used their caste name with their names. They did not want to reveal their identity through names. Influence of education could be seen here also.

More than 75 per cent of the daughters and one third of the mothers had membership in caste organisations. It may be noted that, due to lack of education, the elder generation was unaware of the advantages of caste organisations.

The majority of daughters and mothers were married at the age of 15 or below. The study revealed that the attitude of the Scheduled Caste women towards marriage was changing. As is well known, child marriage had been a dominant norm of the Scheduled Caste community in the past. The situation has undergone change. The daughter respondents have preferred a higher age for marriage for their boys and girls. The educated respondents tended to suggest higher age at marriage for their sons and daughters, when compared to the illiterate and the less educated respondents.

A significant finding of the study was that, there was attitudinal difference, to a greater extent, between the two generations and education was found to be the most important factor in guiding the attitude of the respondents towards various issues. Attitude towards the arrangement of marriage was undergoing change. Though most of the respondents in traditional occupation and elder age group favoured their childrens marriage to be arranged only by the parents, the younger age group and the highly educated respondents were of the opinion that the marriage should be settled by the parents in consultation with the children. Almost all the respondents in the two generations were found to be more in favour of divorce and widow remarriage and were against payment of dowry. Majority of the mothers and daughters favoured endogamous marriage, but as the level of education increased, the tendency to insist on endogamous marriage decreased. Higher the level of education, lower was the proportion who opposed intercaste marriages. It was also found that the elder generation preferred cross cousin marriage more than the younger generation.

Majority of the mother respondents lived in extended families while majority of the daughter respondents lived in nuclear families.

In the case of decision-making process in the family, the daughter respondents had better roles than their mothers. With the influence of modern education and modern occupation, the younger generation had become more independent and expressive than their mothers. Cent per cent of the daughter respondents and a large majority of mother respondents had a favourable attitude towards family planning, though very few among both were practicing it. It was found that the educated mothers showed a more favourable attitude towards family planning. These findings proved our fifth hypothesis that there is greater mobility in the attitudes and reactions, of Scheduled Caste women towards many common social issues and education was found to be a major factor contributing to this.

Our study in respect of religious beliefs, practices, and customs of the respondents revealed certain significant facts. It was found that both the generations had faith in god. It was more pronounced among the respondents of Palghat, who worshipped their own deities. In other districts, none of them worshipped separate deities. Only a small percentage of mother respondents had belief in magic and witchcraft. There was change in the customs regarding marriage, child birth, food habits and dress. At present, Scheduled Caste follow almost all the customs practised by the higher castes.

The findings of our study and the arguments proving our hypothesis became more clear in our case study. With the intention of acquiring indepth knowledge into various aspects of social mobility, two cases were selected from Trivandrum district. In these two cases mobility in areas of education, occupation and intercaste relations and social status, between three generations ie., grandmother, mother and daughter could be seen more pronounced. The study pointed out that there was a slow pace mobility within the three generations. In both the cases, there was considerable change in educational level from grand mother to grand daughter. The third generation, had higher education, due to their high level of aspiration, and awareness about welfare measures.

The trend in occupational mobility showed that there is inter-generational vertical occupational mobility. Analysing these cases, we could identify certain factors contributing to Scheduled Caste women's social mobility namely education, changing intercaste relations, change in the attitudes, and in the level of aspiration. Education, modern occupation and the welface schemes of the government were contributing a lot towards changing the socio-cultural attitudes and the life-style of the Scheduled Caste women.

Bibliography

Abrahamson, Mark, *Sociology*, D. Van Nostrand Company, Ltd., Canada, 1969.

Abbasayulu, Y.B., *Scheduled Caste Elite*, Book Links Corporation, Hyderabad, 1978.

Agarwal, Bina, *Change Among India's Harijans*, Review Article, Seminar, 177, 1974.

Agricultural Finance Corporation, *Comprehensive Development Plan for S.C.s in Chittoor Block*, (*Palghat district*), Bombay, 1984.

Ahmed Karuna, "Towards a Study of Education and Social Change", *Economic and Political Weekly*. January, 27, 1979.

Aiya Nagam, V., *The Travancore State Manual*, Government Press, Travancore, 1906.

Aiyappan, A., *Social Revolution in a Kerala Village*, Asia Publishing House. Bombay, 1965.

Alexander, K.C., *Social Mobility in Kerala*, Deccan College, Poona, 1968.

Alexander, K,C., "Changing Status of Pulaya Harijans", *Economic and Political Weekly*, April, 26, 1969.

Ailen, Ross, D., *Hindu Family in its Urban Setting*, University of Toronto, Toronto Press, 1961.

Ambedkar, B.R., *The Untouchables*, Amrit Book Co., New Delhi, 1948.

Ansari, A.Wahid, *The Changing Village in India*, Chetana Publications, New Delhi, 1980.

Asthana, Prathema, *Women's Movement in India*. Vikas Publishing House, New Delhi, 1974.

Augustine S. John, *The Indian Family in Transition*, Vikas Publishing House, New Delhi, 1982.

Awasthy, Abha, *Hindu Marriage in Continuity and Change*, Lucknow Publishing House, Lucknow.

Balakrishnan, K.K., "Economic Development of Harijans", *Kerala Calling*, Vol. 3, No.12, May, 1913.

Balu and Duncan, *The American Occupatianal Structure*, Wiley, New York, 1957.

Bandhopadhyaya, Samaresh, *Foreign Accounts of Marriage in Ancient India*, Firma K.L. Mukhopadyaya, Calcutta, 1973.

Barber, Bernard, *Social Stratification*, Harcourt Brace and Co., New York, 1957.

Basu, Durga, Das, *Commentary on the Constitution of India*, Sarkar and Sons Ltd, Calcutta, 1956.

Beals L. Ralph (et al), *An Introduction to Anthropology*, Mac-Millan Publishing Co., New York, 1971.

Begom, Javarnesa, M.J., "Aiyankali and the Social Awakening Among the Pulayas", *Journal of Kerala Studies*, Vol. VII March-June, September, December, 1980.

Bennur C.S., and Abraham, D.A., "Study of the relationship between socio-economic status and academic achievement of pupils of rural and urban High School, *Journal of Karnataka University*, 1973.

Beteille, Andre, *Caste, Class and Power*, Oxford Unsversity Press, Bombay, 1960.

Bhai, Nirmala, *Hrijan Women in Independent India*, B.R. Publishing Corporation, New Delhi, 1986.

Bharadwaj A.N., *Problems of S.C.s and S.Ts. in India*, Light and Life Publications, New Delhi, 1979.

Biswas Kumar Dipti, "Harijans", Accelerating Economic Development, *Social Welfare*, Vol. XXV, No.4, July 1978.

Blunt, E.A.H., *The Caste System of Northern India*, S. Chand and Co., Delhi, 1969.

Caplow Theodore, *The Sociology of Work*, The Central Book Depot, Allahabad, 1970.

Chandidas, R., "How close to Equality are Scheduled Castes", *Economic and Political Weekly*, Vol. IV, No. 24, June 14, 1969.

Chatterjee, B., "Social Aspects of Family Planning", *The Indian Journal of Social Work*, Vol. XXII, No.2, July 1971.

Chhibbar, V.B., *From Caste to Class*, Associated Publishing House, New Delhi, 1980.

Chauhan, S.K., *Caste, Status aud Power*, Classical Publishing House, New Delhi, 1980.

Cohn, B.S., "Chamar Family in a North Indian Village", *Economic and Political Weekly*, July 1961.

Constitution of India, Eastern Book Company, Lucknow, 1977.

Coser. L.A., *Masters of Sociological Thought*, Harcount Brac Jovanovicl, I.N.C., New York, 1971.

Dak, T.K. Sharma, L. Mehra Savitha, "Changing Correspondence between Caste and Occupation", *The Eastern Anthropologist*, Vol. 37, No. 4, 1984.

Damle, Y.B., "Reference Group Theory with regard to mobility in caste", in Silverberg (ed) *Social Mobility in the Caste System in India*, Mouton, The Hague, 1968.

Desai, I.P., *The Craft of Sociology and other Essays*, Ajantha Publications, New Delhi, 1981.

Dollu Venkateswaralu, "Psychological conflict between Harijans and Upper Class/Middle Class Caste Hindus, A study in A.P., India, *Sociological Bulletin*, Vol. 36, No. 1, March 1987.

Douglass Marry, *Man in Society*, Adults Book Ltd., London, 1964.

D'Souza, Victor, "Changing Status of Scheduled Castes" *Economic weekly*, Vol. XIV, No. 48, December, 1962.

D'Souza, V.S., *Changing Socio-economic Conditions and Employment of Women in India*, in Transactions of Indian Institute of Advanced Study, Simla, Vol. 7, September 1967.

Dubey, S.M., *Social Mobility Among Professions*, Popular Prakashan, Bombay, 1975.

Dubey, S.N., and Chandar Ganesh, B.K., "Administration of Backward Class Hostels in A.P., *Economic and Political Weekly*, Vol. VIII, No. 46, November 17, 1973.

Dubey, S.N., and Mathur Usha, "Welfare Programmes for Scheduled Castes", Content and administration", *Economic and Political Weekly*, Vol. VIII, No. 4, January 22, 1972.

Domont, Louis, *Home Hierarchies*, Vikas Publication, Banglore, 1966.

Duncan, Mitchell (ed)., *The Dictionary of Sociology*, Routledge and Kegan Paul, 1968.

Durkheim, Emile, *The Elementary form of Religious Life*, George Allen and Unwin Ltd., 1955.

Ellis A. Robert, "Social Mobility and Social Isolation", A test of Sorokin's dissociative hypothesis, *American Sociological Review*, Vol. 32, No. 2, April, 1967.

Everett Jana, Lebra Joyce, Paulson Joy, *Women and Work in India, Continuity and Change*, Promilla and Co. Publishers, New Delhi, 1984.

Farooqul Vimala, "Crusade Against Exploitation of Women", *Social Welfare*, Vol. XXIX, No. 5, August, 1982.

Fichter, H. Joseph, *Sociology*, The University of Chicago Press, London, 1971.

Francis, E. Marril and Mabel Elliot, *Social Disorganisation*, Harper and Row Publishers, New York, 1961.

Gelender Marc, "Untouchability and Law", *Economic and Political Weekly*, January, 1969.

Ganguli, B.N., *Social Development*, Sterling Publishing Pvt. Ltd, New Delhi, 1977.

Ghosh, S.K., *Protection of Minorities and Scheduled Castes*, Ashish Publishing House, New Delhi, 1980.

Ginnis Mc. R., "A Scholastic Model of Social Mobility', *American Sociological Review*, No. 33 (5), 1968.

Gore, M.S., *Urbanisation and Family Change*, Popular Prakashan, Bombay, 1968.

Gough, P. Kathleen, *Social and Religious Change in Central Kerala*, M.N. Srinivas, (ed) "In India's Village' Asia Publishing House, Bombay, 1960.

Government of India, *Reports of the Commissioner for Scheduled Castes and Scheduled Tribes*, 1962 to 1963, Manager of Publication, New Delhi.

Government of India, *Reports of the Commissioner for Schedul-ed Tribes*, 1965, Manager of Publication, New Delhi.

Government of India, *Reports of the Commissioner for Scheduled Castes and Scheduled Tribes*, 1971, 1972, Manager of Publications, New Delhi.

Government of India, *Reports of the Scheduled Caste and Scheduled Tribes*, Commission, Ministry of Home Affairs, 1967.

Government of India, *Womens' Developments, some critical issues*, Marvah Publications, New Delhi, 1978.

Government of Kerala. *Annual Administration Report*, Scheduled Caste Development Department, 1986-87.

Government of Kerala, *Report of Commissioner on the Socio-economic Conditions of Scheduled Castes and Scheduled Tribes*, Vol. I to V, Part I, 1982.

Government of Kerala, "Study of Educated Unemployed Scheduled Castes and Scheduled Tribes in Kerala", *Man Power Division*, Dept. of Economics and Statistics, November, 1983.

Goyal, B.R., *Educating Harijans*, The Academic Press, India, 1981.

Goyal, O.P., *Caste and Voting Behaviour*, Ritu Publishers, New Delhi, 1981.

Goode, William, *The Family*, Prentice Hall of India, Pvt. Ltd., New Delhi, 1965.

Green W. Arnold, *Sociology*, (IVth edition), McGraw Hill Book Co., New York, 1964.

Gulati, Leela, *Profiles in Female Poverty*, Hindusthan Publishing Corporation, New Delhi, 1981.

Gulati, Leela, "Profile of a Female Agriculture Labourer", *Working Paper 53*, Centre for Development Studies, August, 1977.

Gulati, Leela, "Sex descrimination in farm wages", *Working Paper 44*, Centre for Development Studies, November, 1976.

Gulati, Leela, "Women in unorganised sector" with special reference to Kerala, *Working Paper*, 172, Centre for Development Studies, 1982.

Hutton J.H., *Caste in India*, Oxford University Press, 1977.

Horton B. Paul (et. al), *Sociology*, McGraw Hill, Kogakusha Ltd., Tokyo, 1976.

Indira Awasthy, *Rural Women of India*, B.R. Publishing Corporation, Delhi, 1982.

Isaacs, R. Harold, *India's Ex-untouchables*, Asia Publishing House, Bombay, 1965.

Iyer Anantha Krishna, *Social History of Kerala*, Vol. II. Book Centre Publications, Madras, 1968.

Iyer Anantha Krishna, L.K., *Tribes and Castes of Cochin*, Vol. I, Cosmo Publications, New Delhi, 1981.

Jablow Alta and Hammund Dorothy, *Women: Their Familial Roles in Traditional Societies*, University of New York, A Cummings Module in Anthropology, No. 57.

Jetley, S., "Education and Occupational Mobility.', *Economic and Political Weekly*, Vol. IV, No.17, April 26, 1969.

Kagzi, M.C.J., *Segregation and Untouchability Abolition*, Metropolitan Book Co., Pvt. Ltd., New Delhi, 1976.

Kamble, N.C., *Atrocities on Scheduled Castes in Post Independent India*, Ashih Publishing House, New Delhi, 1981.

Kamble, N.D., *The Scheduled Castes*, Ashih Publishing House, New Delhi, 1982.

Kamble, N.D., *Deprived Castes and their struggle for Equality*, Ashish Publishing House, New Delhi, 1983.

Kananaikil Josc, "Marginalisation of the Scheduled Castes", A Sociological Interpretation, *Social Action*, Vol. 32 No. 3, July, September, 1982.

Kannan, C.T., *Intercaste and Inter Community Marriages in* India, Allied Publishers (Pvt.) Bombay, 1963.

Kannan C.T., *Interracial Marriages in London*, S.W. Litho Printers Ltd., London, 1972.

Kapoor Ravi, *Education and Social Stratification in South East Asia*, Idarah-i Adabiyat-i-Delhi, 1985.

Kapadia, K.M., *Marriage and Family in India*, Indian Branch, Oxford University Press, London, 1958,

Kapoor Promilla, *Woman in the Home in Kamala Bhasin* (ed.) *Position of Women in India*, Fredarick Nauhman Stiffing, Bombay, 1972.

Karleker *Malavika*, "Some Perspective on the Employment of Scheduled Caste Women", *Social Action*, Indian Social Institute, Vol. 32 No. 3 July, September 1982.

Kaushik Susheela, *Woman's Oppression*, Shakti Books, New Delhi, 1985.

Khan Mumtaz Ali, "Impact of the Constitutional Protection and Safeguards on the S.C. of Santhur Village", *Economic Review*, May 15 Vol. 20, 1969.

Khan Mumtaz Ali, *Scheduled Castes and their status in India*, Uppal Publishing House, New Delhi, 1980.

Khan Mumtaz Ali and Aysha Noor, *Status of Rural Women*, Uppal Publishing House, New Delhi, 1982.

Kirpal Viney, "Higher Education for the Scheduled Castes and Scheduled Tribes", *Economic and Political Weekly*, Vol. XIII, Nos. 4 and 5, January 28 February 4, 1978.

Koshy, M.J., "Political Awakening and Struggle for Freedom in Travancore", *Journal of Indian History*, University of Kerala, Serial No. 149, Vol. L. Part II, August, 1972.

Kumari Shantha, *Scheduled Caste and Welfare Measures*, Classical Publishing Company, New Delhi, N.D.

Kunjaman, "Emergence of a slave caste Pulaya", Book Review, *Journal of Kerala Studies*, Vol. VII, March-Decem. 1980.

Lalithamma, "Some Factors Affecting Achievement of Secondary School Pupils in Mathematics", *Research Review, Journal* Kerala University, Vol. I, 1976.

Lekshmi Anantha, *The Generation Gap, The Indian Family in* the Change and Challenge of the Seventees", Sterling Publishers, New Delhi, 1272.

Linton Ralph, *The Study of Man*, Har Court Brace and Co., New York, 1963.

Lipset, S.M. and Zatterberg, H.L., *A Theory of Social Mobility in Class Status, Power*, edited by Lipset and Bendix, Free Press, New York, 1966.

Lipset, S.M. and Bendix Reinhard, *Social Mobility in Industrial Society*, University of California Press, London. 1967

Lopreato Joseph, "Upward Social Mobility and Political Orientation", *American Socialogical Review*, Vol. No. 32, No. 4, August, 1967.

Luthra, P.N., "Equality to Women in the Social Set Up", *Social Welfare*, Vol. XXII, No. 3, June, 1975.

Mahajan, O.P., Women and Labour Laws, *Social Welfare*, Vol. XXVIII, No. 5, August 1981.

Majumdar, D.N., *Report on the Sociological Status of Caste and Tribes of Gujarat*", 1950.

Malik Suneila, *Social Integration of Scheduled Caster*, Abhinav Publications, New Delhi, 1979.

Mani, K.M., and Balakrishnan, K.K., "Economic Development on Harijans", *Kerala Calling*, Department of Public Relations, Vol. 13, No.12, May, 1973.

Mani, K.M., Emphasis on Development of Individual, *Kerala Calling*, Department of Public Relations, Vol. 4 No.J, May, 1984.

Manohar Murali, *Socio Economic Status of Indian Women*, Seema Publication, Delhi, 1983.

Marriot, Mc.Kin, *Village India*, The University of Chicago Press, London, 1963.

Mathur, S.S., *A Sociological Approach to Indian Education*, Vinod Pustak Mandir, Agra, 1966.

Mathur, K-S., Shukla B.R.K. Singh Bhanvir, *Studies in Social Change*, Ethanographer and Folk Culture Society, Lucknow, 1973.

Mathew, Minnie, "A New Approach to Harijan and Girijan Development", *Kerala Calling*, Public Relations, Vol. 4, No. 7, May, 1984.

Mazumdar Vina, *Rolc of Rural Women in Development*, Allied Publishers, Pvt. Ltd., Bombay, 1978.

Mc Roberts A., Hugh and Kevin Selbee, "Trends in Occupational Mobility", *American Sociological Review*, Vol. 56, No. 4, August, 1981.

Mehta, S.R., 'Acceptance of Change", *Social Change*, Council for Sacial Development, Vol. 13, No. 1, March, 1983.

Mehta Sushila, *Revolution and Status of Women in India*, Metropolitan Book Co. (P) Ltd., New Delhi, 1982.

Mehra Savitha, *Social Mobility in Rural Haryana*. Ph.D. Thesis, Haryana University, Hissar, 1982.

M. Kumar Indu, *Education and Social Status of Muslim Women in Kerala*, Ph.D. Thesis, University of Kerala, Trivandrum, 1976.

Menon, Indu, *Status of Muslim Women in India*, Uppal Publishing House, New Delhi, 1981.

Merton, R.K., *Social Theory and Social Structure*, Free Press, Illinois, 1949.

Mies Maria, "Class Struggle of Emancipation", *Economic and Political Weekly*, Vol. VIII, No. 50, December 15, 1973.

Mohan, P.E., *History of the Harijan*, (*Scheduled Caste Uplift in Tamil Nadu*) 1900-1955), Ph.D. Thesis, University of Madras, Madras, 1983.

Moni Sarada, K., *Emergence of a Slave Caste*, People's Publishing House, New Delhi, 1980.

Moni Sarada, K., *Divided the Poor*, Ajantha Publications, New Delhi, 1981.

Moni Sarada, K. (ed), *Women, Work and Society*, Indian Statistical Institute, Calcutta, 1985.

Murdock, G.P., *Social Structure*, MacMillan Co., New York, 1949.

Murthy, B.S., *Depressed and Opressed*, S. Chand Co., New Delhi, 1972.

Naidu, S. Usha, "Socialisation of Scheduled Caste Children at School', *Social Change*, Council for Social Development Vol. 19 No. 4, December, 1979.

Naik Pat Sidhartha, *Education and Social Mobility in India*, An attempt at Analysis from Neo-Webariand Perspective. Ph.D. Thesis, Jawaharlal Nehru Univesity, New Delhi, 1978.

Narayana, D., "A Note on Occupational Mobilty", Caste and job reservation", *Working Paper No. 137*, Centre for Development Studies, Prasanth Nagar, Trivandrum.

Nayar, P.K.B., *Development of Kerala, Problems and Promises,* Dept. of Sociology Publications, University of Kerala, 1972.

Nayar, P.K.B., "Family as a Determinant of Women's Social Status", *Kerala Sociologist*, Vol. XIII, No. 2, July-December, 1985.

Nijhawan, N.K., "Occupational Mobility and Political Development', *Economic and Political Weekly*, Annual No. Vol. No. VI, No. 3, 4, 5, January 1971.

Obrien. W. Robert, (et.al), "*Readings in General Sociology*, Houghton Mifflin Co., Bosten, 1951.

Omvedt, Gail, We Shall Smash the Prison Some Day", *The Illustrated weekly of India*, April 8 to 14, 1984.

Oommen, T.K., "Strategy for Social Change", A study on untouchability, *Economic and Political Weekly* Vol. III, No. 35, June, 1968.

Oommen, M.A., *Kerala Economy Since Independence*, Oxford and IBH Publishing Co., New Delhi, 1979.

Ottaway, A.K.C., *Education and Society*, Routledge and Kegan Paul, The Humanity's Press, New York, 1960.

Pandey, "Seven Years of Change", Book Review, *Indian Journal of Social Work*, No. 41, 1980.

Paranjpe, *Caste, Prejudice and the Individual*, Publishing House, Bombay, 1970.

Parthasarathy, *Rural Population in Indian Urban City*, B.R. Publishing Corporation, New Delhi, 1984.

Parvathamma, "The Weaker Sections of India". 'The Scheduled Castes in India', *Sociological Bulletin*, Vol. No. 30, No. 1, March 1981.

Parvathamma, C., Paper presented at the Parliamentary Forum, *S.C. and S.T.*, New Delhi, 1973.

Patwardhan Sunantha, *Change Among Indias Harijans*, Orient Longman, New Delhi, 1973.

Phadmis Urmila, Malani India, *Women of the World, Illusion and Reality*, Vikas Publishing House, New Delhi, 1978.

Pillai Narayana, G., *Development of Social Welfare in Kerala*, New Delhi, 1979.

Pillai, Velu, T.K., *Travancore State Manual*, Vol. 3, The Government of Travancore, Trivandrum, 1940.

Prabhu, P.N., *Report of the Seminar on Casteism and Removal of Untouchadillty*, Published by Indian Conference of Social Work, Bombay, 1955.

Premi K. Kusum, "Education for the Weak", *Yojana*, Vol. 28 No. 17, September 16-30, 1984.

Rachan, A. Rosenfield, "Women's Intergenerational Occupational Mobility", *American Sociological* Review, Vol. 43, 1978.

Raja Gopalan, C., *Social Mobility among Scheduled Castes*, Report of I.C.S.S.R., Bangalore University, Bangolore, 1978.

Ralph, Turner, "In Role Taking, Role Stand Point and Reference Group Behaviour", *American Journal of Sociology*, 1956.

Rama Chandran, P., *Some Aspects of Labour Mobility in Bombay City*, Tata Institute of Social Science Series, Somaiya Publications Pvt. Ltd., New Delhi, 1974.

Ram, Nanda, *The Mobile Scheduled Castes*, Hindusthan Publishing corporation New Delhi, 1988.

Rao, M.S.A., *Tradition, Rationality and Change*, Popular Prakashan, Bombay, 1972.

Rao, M.S.A., *Social Movements and Social Transformation*, Macmillan and Company of India Limited, New Delhi, 1979.

Rao, M.S.A., Social Movements in India, (Peasant and Backward Class Movements), Vol. I, Manohar Publications, New Delhi, 1978.

Rao Usha, N.J., *Depressed Castes in India*, Chugh Publications, Allahabad, 1981.

Rao Usha, N.J. *Women in a Developing Society*, Ashish Publishing House, New Delhi, 1983.

Rayappa Hanumantha, and Grover Deepak, *Employment Planning for the Rural Poor*, Sterling Publishers Pvt. Ltd., Bangalore, 1980.

Reddy Narayan Karan, V., *Man, Education and Values*, B.R. Publishing Corporation, Delhi, 1979.

Report of Department of Public Relations, "More Concessions to Harijans", *Kerala Calling*, Vol. 3, No. 6, November, 1982.

Richard, A.Hall, *Occupation and Social Structure*, Prentice Hall 1969.

Richard Lannoy, *The Speaking Tree*, Oxford University Press, London, 1971.

Roy Chandra Girish, *Indian Culture, The Tradition of Non-violence and Social Change in India*, Ajanta Publications, New Delhi, 1976.

Roy Rama Shray and Singh, V.B., *A Study of Harijan Elites*, Sangita Printers, New Delhi, 1987.

Saberwal, Satheesh, "Preceding Pollution', Intercaste Relations in Urban Punjab", *Sociological Bullettin*, Vol. 22, No. 2, 1973.

............"Blacks, Harijans and Muslims', *Economic and Political Weekly*, Vol. VIII, No. 41, October 1973.

Sachidananda, *The Harijan Elite*, Thomson Press Ltd. India 1977.

Saksena, H.S., *Safeguards for Scheduled Castes and Tribes*, Uppal Publishing House, New Delhi, 1981.

Sampatram, "Tribal and Harijan Welfare", *Social Welfare*, Vol. XXIX, No. 7, October, 1982.

Satya Narayana and Parvathamma, *New Horizons and Scheduled Castes*, Ashish Publishing House, New Delhi, 1984.

Selbia Kevin, and McRoberts Hugh, "Trends in Occupational Mobility", *American Sociological Review*, No. 4, Vol. 46, August, 1981.

Seliitz Claire et. al., *Research Methods in Social Relations*, Methuen and Co., Ltd., U.S.A, 1959.

Senart Emile, *Caste in India*, E.S.S. Publication, Delhi, 1975.

Sergeant Graham, *A Text Book of Sociology*, MacMillan Education Ltd., London, 1978.

Sethi Mohini Raj, *Modernisation of Working Women in Developing Societies*, National Publishing House, New Delhi, 1976.

Sharma, A.M., "Agriculture Labour Union in South Indian States", Book Review, *Indian Journal of Social of Work*, Vol. XLI, No. 4, 1980.

Shah, A.B., *Higher Education and Development*, Association of Indian Universities, Golden Jubilee Seminar, New Delhi, 1975.

Shakir Moin, *Politics and Minorities*, Ajanta Publications, New Delhi, 1980.

Sharda Bam Dev, *Status attainment in rural India*, Ajanta Publications, Delhi, 1977.

Sharma, K.L., "Levels of Mobility in Caste structure", *Indian Journal of Social Work*, January, 1972.

Sharma, K.Z., *Essays on Social Stratification*, Rawat Publications, Jaipur, 1980.

Sharma, S.S., "Untouchability, Myth or Reality", *Sociological Bullettin*, Vol. 35, March, 1986.

Sharma, Radha Krishna, *Nationalism, Social Reforms and Indian Women*, Janaki Prakashan, Patna, 1981.

Showeb, M., *Education and Mobility among Harijans*, Gandhian Institute, Varanasi, 1983.

Shukla, N.K., *The Social Structure of an Indian Village*, Cosmo Publications, India, 1976.

Sinha, Arun, 'Class War" 'Not atrocities against Harijans", *Economic and Political Weekly*, Vol. XII, No. 50, December 10, 1970.

Sinha, Reghuvir, *Social Change in Indian Society*, Progressive Publishers, Bhopal, 1975.

Singh, Harindar, *Caste Among Non-Hinduism India*, National Publishing House, New Delhi, 1977.

Singh, Mohendar, *The Depressed Classes*, Hind Kitabs Ltd., Bombay, 1947.

Singh Soran, *Scheduled Castes of India*, Gain Publishing House, Delhi, 1987.

Singh, Tarlock, *Poverty and Social Change*, Orient Longman's regional office, New Delhi.

Sinha, R.K., *Alienation Among Scheduled Castes*, Manas Publications, Delhi, 1986.

Slocum, L. Walter, *Occupational Careers*, Aldine Pnblishing Company, Chicago, 1968.

Sorokin, P.A., *Social and Cultural Mobility*, Free Press, America, 1927.

Sorokin, P.A., *Contemporary Sociological Theories*, Harper and Row Publishers, New York, 1964.

Srinivas, M.N., *Marriage and Family in Mysore*", New Book Co., 1942.

Srinivas, M.N., *Religion and Society Among Coorgs of South India*, Allied Publishers, Bombay, 1952.

Srinivas, M.N., "A note on Sanskritization and Westernisation", *The far Eastern Quarterly*, No. 15, 1956.

Srinivas, M.N., *Social Change in Modern India*, University of Colifornia Press, Berkely, 1966.

Srinivas, M.N., *Dimensions of Social Change in India*, Allied Publishers Pvt. Ltd., Bombay, 1977.

Thurston, Edgar, *Caste and Tribes of Southern India*, Vol. IV, Cosmo Publications, New Delhi, 1975.

Trivedi R. Harshad, *Scheduled Caste Women*, Concept Publishing Company, New Delhi, 1977.

Vagiswari, *Income Earning Trends and Social Status of the Harijan Community in Tamil Nadu*, Sangham Publishers, Madras, 1972.

Vatsa Singh Rajendra, *The Depressed Classes of India*, Githanjali Prakashan, New Delhi, 1977.

Venkata Ratnam, *Social Mobility of Scheduled Castes in Madurai District*, Madurai Kamaraj University, Madurai, 1981.

Victor D' Souza, "Changing status of Scheduled Castes", *Economic and Political Weekly*, Vol. XVI, Bombay, 1962.

Vidyarthi, L.P., "Position and Problems of Scheduled Castes in Bihar", *The Eastern Anthropologist*, Vol. 37, No. 3, July-September, 1984.

Vidyarthi, L.P., N. Mishra, *Harijan Today,* Classical Publications, New Delhi, 1977.

Yadev, S.K., *Harijan Awareness of educational schemes*, The Academic Press, Harayana, 1983.

Index